MW00603348

Katherine

Thank you for being a
great partner!
I hope you enjoy the Book

Good Selling

PRAISE FOR

THE SUCCESS CADENCE

"THE SUCCESS CADENCE offers a significant set of
ing competitive advantages to any sales leader in any spac
read stuff."

—**ANKUR KOTHARI,** Co-Fou
Chief Revenue Officer, Automation A

"David, Tom, and Bart give us the practical actions tha
winning organization from the individual up. With their
focus on securing people who are willing and able, the autl
all of us how to create enduring value."

—**ALEX SHOOTMAN,** CEO, \

"The best source of wisdom on rapid business growth curr
able in book form."

—**RAJESH RAM,** Chief Customer Offi

"Mattson, Schodorf, and Fanelli really understand how
of a successful sales machine works. THE SUCCESS C
breaks down the systems and processes that drive rap
growth, demystifying them once and for all, and pass
simple, practical model that virtually any sales team can be

—**ANDRE DURAND,** CEO, P

THE
SUCCESS
CADENCE^{SM}

UNLEASH
Your Organization's
RAPID GROWTH CULTURE

**DAVID MATTSON,
TOM SCHODORF & BART FANELLI**

© 2019 Sandler Systems, Inc., Tom Schodorf, and Bart Fanelli. All rights reserved.

Reproduction, modification, storage in a retrieval system or retransmission, in any form or by any means, electronic, mechanical, or otherwise, is strictly prohibited without the prior written permission of Sandler Systems, Inc.

S Sandler Training (with design), Sandler, and Sandler Selling System are registered service marks of Sandler Systems, Inc.

Success Cadence is a jointly owned service mark of Sandler Systems, Inc., Tom Schodorf, and Bart Fanelli.

Hardback: 978-0-578-49810-2

E-book: 978-0-578-49811-9

Contents

Part 2: The Calendar Matters

Part 3: From Slow Growth to Rapid Growth

Acknowledgments

MY DEEP GRATITUDE GOES OUT to the many clients, strategic partners, and Sandler® employees and franchisees who supported and encouraged us as we wrote this book. In addition, I'd like to thank my two endlessly resourceful coauthors. I must also thank Steve Tchejeyan at Symantec, Mark Roberge of the Harvard Business School, Adam Miller of Cornerstone, and the far-flung members of the Sandler team—Yusuf Toropov, Rachel Miller, Lori Ames, Margaret Stevens Jacks, Jennifer Willard, Laura Matthews, Brian Sullivan, Jerry Dorris, Deborah Jordan, Jasmine Stephens, Elizabeth Faust, Jena Heffernan, Sarah Prokopchak, Denni Griffith, and Désirée Pilachowski—all of whom made invaluable contributions to this project.

— David Mattson

I HAVE TO BEGIN WITH my father, Otto Schodorf, to whom I dedicate this book. He was that rare man who never considered himself to be a leader, but who was a great leader nevertheless. As I look back on this project, and the support I received while working on it, I am deeply grateful to my mother Beth Schodorf, who taught me the importance of patience, fortitude, and an even temperament; to my wife Patty, who has supported me unconditionally through the ups and downs of seven moves and the long emotional roller-coaster of a sales and executive management career; to my four brothers Bill, Joe, Steve, and Greg, who taught me common sense and the

v

ways of the world; to my children Ali and Andi from whom I have learned more than they will ever know; to my two patient and innovative coauthors; to the members of the Sandler team, notably Yusuf Toropov and Laura Matthews, for their help in editing the text, and Lori Ames, for her insights on positioning it; to David Hornik of August Capital; to Richard Wiktor, Dave Buckles, and Jerry Lowe at IBM; to Clarissa Cruz, Walter Scott, John Pullen, Debbie Tummins, Becky Fuller, Jay Gardner, Kathy Bexley, the late Elizabeth Hueben, and most especially Bob Beauchamp at BMC; to Fred Vocolla at Kaseya; to Jason Ewell at Insight Venture Partners; to Mark Stouse at Proof Analytics; to John Connors at Ignition Partners; to Steve Rowland at DataStax; to Paulo Rosado at Outsystems; to Jill Rowley at Stage 2 Capital; to James Murray; to Ankur Kothari and Mihir Shukla; to Garry Kasparov; to Rajesh Ram at Egnyte; to Alex Shootman at Workfront, whose integrity and uncompromising ethics have enabled him to serve as such a powerful role model to me and to countless others; to Stephanie Furfaro and Corey Thomas at Rapid7, and to Corey specifically for teaching me the value of grace, collaboration, and sense of humor around opinionated constituencies; to Dave Conte and the late Steve Sommer at Splunk; to Godfrey Sullivan at Splunk, who taught me leadership principles that continue to inspire me today; and to Douglas Merritt, President and CEO of Splunk, for turning any number of dreams into reality.

—Tom Schodorf

I'D LIKE TO BEGIN THIS note of gratitude by dedicating the book to my mom Mary Gallo, my dad Frank Fanelli, and my sister Maria

Schmidt, who I know are now watching over me from the ether. My personal thanks for providing invaluable help on the project goes out to Yusuf Toropov and Laura Matthews, to Dave Mattson for believing in me and embracing an idea that no one else had put forward; to Tom Schodorf for being my ultimate champion, for placing his trust in me, and for inspiring me to pursue an entrepreneurial path; to everyone Tom mentioned above; to Sidney Sack, my first coach and mentor in business, for teaching me that there are no limits to personal and organizational achievement; to Steve Rowland, who knew that it was "all about we"; to Dave Conte, who disproved the myth that Sales and Finance are mutually exclusive; and to Erica, Dominic, Luca, and Rocco, for grounding me in "family first," and supporting me throughout our personal and professional journey.

—Bart Fanelli

Introduction

IS THERE A STRATEGY YOU can count on to deliver rapid, "hockey stick" growth to your company? We believe that there is, and that it rests on a strategic decision to invest in your sales team.

Today's sales leaders live in an extraordinary period—a period when the data-driven tools available to them and to those who report to them are richer and more adaptable than ever. We can and should take advantage of those tools to increase the velocity of the sales process and to reduce the amount of time spent handling mundane, repetitive tasks. In the final analysis, however, rapid, aggressive company growth means ramping up our investment in the right human beings.

Sales is, after all, all about building and supporting personal business relationships—and high-performing salespeople are the means by which such relationships are created and sustained. Although automation has the capacity to accelerate the sales process, we don't see a situation emerging any time soon where software alone will create and support one-on-one relationships with senior-level decision makers. You need top-tier salespeople for that. If your objective is rapid, scalable growth, you need to target such salespeople, recruit them, hire them, support them, and ramp them up to full capacity quickly.

This book sets out a viable plan for doing just that. In Part 1, "Laying the Foundation," you learn what your real job as a sales leader is. In Part 2, "The Calendar Matters," you find out how to establish and sustain the unique organizational rhythm of a rapid-growth sales culture. Finally, in Part 3, "From Slow Growth to Rapid Growth," you get insights on how to overcome the most common obstacles to launching and supporting "hockey stick" revenue growth. As you will see, the focus throughout is on people, starting with you and the members of your team. And by the way, even if yours is already a high-performing company, the ideas we share in the following pages will help your team to perform at an even higher level.

Let's get started!

Part 1:
Laying the Foundation

CHAPTER ONE

The Growth Paradox

THIS IS A BOOK ABOUT:

- moving out of your personal and organizational comfort zone ...
- to create and sustain the distinctive operational cadence for yourself and your team ...
- which will deliver a rapid-growth sales culture when combined with the right methodology and toolkit.

The rapid-growth culture you will be reading about here has been tested and proven to work. Among other places, it has worked at Splunk, a company founded in 2003 that had raised $40 million in venture capital funding by 2007 and that broke the billion-dollar revenue mark in 2018. As we send this book to press, the company is tracking for close to $2 billion in annual revenue and $20 billion in market valuation. That's rapid growth. Yes, it's connected to a great product—a product that offers corporate leaders meaningful insights, via easy-to-use, customized dashboards, into otherwise impenetrable data generated from a range of security technologies. But that astonishing growth trajectory isn't just because of all the great things that Splunk products do.

Your company's growth is attributable to the rhythm of its sales team. You can accelerate that growth by adopting the scalable cultural and leadership process you'll be learning here. We call the team rhythm that predictably delivers rapid revenue growth the *Success Cadence*. That rhythm is learnable, repeatable, and sustainable—when it's modeled at the top.

Here is what rapid-growth Success Cadence revenue performance looks like when you chart it on a graph:

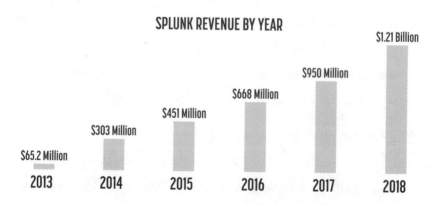

SPLUNK REVENUE BY YEAR

$65.2 Million	$303 Million	$451 Million	$668 Million	$950 Million	$1.21 Billion
2013	2014	2015	2016	2017	2018

Rapid revenue growth is possible and sustainable, regardless of your industry and your current position in the marketplace, if you are willing to change your thinking and your behaviors. This book aims to show you how to do that by consciously designing a clear daily, weekly, monthly, and quarterly operational cadence for yourself and your sales team.

> *"Achieving and maintaining hypergrowth at Splunk has happened as a result of relentless focus on customer outcomes, selecting and executing on a few key initiatives at a time, and investing heavily in customer facing personnel. We've found that a great product in combination with strong and well funded go-to-market teams enable us to innovate at a rapid pace, bringing differentiated value to market for the benefit of our customers, partners, employees, and shareholders."*

–DOUG MERRITT, PRESIDENT AND CEO, SPLUNK

Even a Great Product Needs a Great Sales Team

How do you scale aggressive sales growth consistently? How do you achieve rapid, dramatic growth in your company—and sustain that growth over time? Is there really a viable, repeatable process for doing this?

The answers to these important questions are all waiting to be found within a paradox that every sales leader who ends up delivering rapid, sustainable revenue growth eventually encounters—and masters. The paradox is: Your product is not your product.

The aggressive, sustainable growth so many company leaders seek, but few can actually point to, lies in moving yourself and your organization into a sales culture.

Moving into a sales culture means acknowledging, first and foremost to yourself, that no matter how great your product is, no matter how wonderful its design, no matter how far ahead of the curve you may believe it to be, your product is not great enough to sell itself. If it were, you wouldn't be reading this book. While some companies have attempted product-led growth with decent results, the reality remains that anything that is sold needs a sales team and any sales team needs both a clear leader and a clear process.

> We've worked with many people over the years who came up through the sales ranks and who have held a variety of positions in different functions in their career, including R&D. The pattern we've noticed is that they've come to the same conclusion that we have: In the end, if we want to be successful, we all "work" for sales.

Thus, the creation of the most cutting-edge product imaginable does not guarantee success, or even survival, in the marketplace. Just ask Sony about Betamax, the cutting-edge videotape format launched in the mid-1970s that had better image quality and better sound than the rival VHS format that emerged to challenge it. It's a complex story, one with lots of moving parts, but the ending is what matters. While Sony won the design battle (because, on paper, it had the technologically more advanced product), it stumbled in terms of positioning, marketing, and sales—and lost the war for marketplace dominance.

*"I've been fortunate in my career to have a number of functional roles,
at the contributor as well as executive level. Due primarily to its
intimacy with customer pain, and the understanding of the value of
the solutions that addressed that pain, none of those roles prepared me
more for being a leader and ultimately for being a CEO, than sales."*

—ROBERT BEAUCHAMP, CEO AND PRESIDENT, BMC SOFTWARE

That's a classic cautionary tale in business, but it is one whose most important moral is often overlooked. The Betamax story suggests that leaders may sometimes need to change the way they think about what the product really is.

For instance: If your company sells software, you may be used to thinking of your product as software. If your company sells engineering services, you may be used to thinking of your product as engineering. If your company sells consulting, you may be used to thinking of your product as consulting. But if you are going to establish true leadership of your sales team, if you are going to scale your company's growth over time, you need to understand that the physical objects and the services you ask salespeople to sell aren't really your product.

As a sales leader, you must understand that your product is actually salespeople who are both *willing* and *able* to do their job. (You'll see the phrase "willing and able" a lot in this book. We'll be exploring it in depth throughout.)

That's what you are really being paid to find, develop, and bring into the organization. That's what you are paid to hold onto. That's what will determine whether or not your growth curve is scalable: salespeople who are both willing and able to do their job.

"We look for companies that have demonstrated some product market fit, and we then work with them to improve their position in the markets they serve. To reach their full potential and achieve extraordinary returns for their investors and employees alike, companies need to instill accountability within and across functions, and the best place to drive accountability, both from the inside out and the outside in, is sales."

—DAVID HORNIK, GENERAL PARTNER, AUGUST CAPITAL

Salespeople who are both willing and able are the ultimate competitive advantage—and finding them, hiring them, and holding onto them must be your top priority.

Key Takeaways

- Aggressive, sustainable sales growth lies in moving yourself and your organization out of a product culture—and into a sales culture.
- Salespeople who are both willing and able are the ultimate competitive advantage—and finding them, hiring them, and holding onto them must be your top priority.

CHAPTER TWO

Willing and Able

THE SINGLE MOST CRITICAL RESPONSIBILITY of sales leaders is to assemble a sales team with members who are both willing and able to do their jobs and who are closely connected to the customer.

Everything sales leaders learn and do in order to scale their team's success comes from their salespeople's willingness and ability to both understand and act on customers' (and prospective customers') experience.

To make what we're talking about here just a little clearer, consider a fundamental element of the job description of a salesperson who's responsible for generating new client relationships: prospecting. How many sales leaders have faced the challenge of having a salesperson on staff who clearly understood the problems their product or service solved, who understood how to add value to someone's day, who was technically able to do the behaviors that would allow them to develop a base of new business opportunities—but who was, for some reason, consistently unwilling to prospect for business at the level the role required?

Anyone who has ever led a sales team has had that experience. The big question with such a salesperson is whether you can coach them from the lower-right quadrant to the upper-right quadrant of the matrix shown below.

WILLING AND UNABLE	WILLING AND ABLE
UNWILLING AND UNABLE	UNWILLING AND ABLE

If you can't coach, support, and lead such salespeople in a way that inspires them to move their daily and weekly routine from "unwilling and able" to "willing and able," not just in terms of prospecting but in every critical area, then guess what? You're not doing your organization, your team, or your own career any favors by keeping the person in a sales role. Not only that—you're also failing to deliver the product that makes sustainable, scalable growth possible: salespeople who are both willing and able.*

Of course, it's natural for there to be some movement back and

---

* We don't limit this viewpoint to salespeople only. The willing-and-able revolution typically starts in the sales team and then extends across the company. In terms of growing revenue aggressively, there are definitely certain roles—such as technical support—where the same level of commitment is going to be essential. In the best case, everyone in the organization, including senior executives, will use the willing-and-able coaching and assessment model identified here.

forth between these quadrants. For instance, when you introduce a brand-new product line, even your best salespeople are going to be unable to sell it at first, no matter how willing they may be, because they don't yet know enough about the product to message about it or discuss the value it delivers with prospects. A salesperson who is going through a personal crisis at home may fall behind and find themself temporarily unable and unwilling to do the job. But these are typically transitional events. They don't define entire careers. The key question is the direction, the trajectory, in which the person (and by extension the entire team) is moving over time. Is the salesperson moving up and to the right? Are they able to adapt seamlessly to new products and capabilities, new prospecting tools, new selling strategies, additional buyers, higher level buyers, multiple product lines, or even an entirely new selling model? The answer needs to be *yes*—and the rest of the team and, eventually, the entire company also needs to be able—because you have to assume that your competition is.

Consider that salesperson who is consistently stuck in the lower-right quadrant of the matrix when it comes to, say, prospecting. Whose issue is that really? The sales leader's. Why? Because they hired that salesperson! And it's the leader's job to move them up—or out.

Key Takeaways

- Everything you learn and do in order to scale your team's success comes from the salesperson's willingness and ability to both understand and act on the customers' (and prospective customers') experience.

- The key question is the direction, the trajectory, in which the person (and by extension the entire team) is moving over time. Is the salesperson moving up and to the right—toward "willing and able"?

CHAPTER THREE

The Success Trajectory

GIVEN THAT SALESPEOPLE WHO ARE both willing and able to do their jobs is the real product that you as a sales leader are responsible for delivering—and given that you want to deliver scalable growth for your organization—you have to start asking yourself some tough questions.

- "Who am I hiring?"
- "Why am I hiring them?"
- "Who am I trying to keep?"
- "Why am I trying to keep them?"

We believe the best answer to all those questions can be found in a single word: *trajectory*.

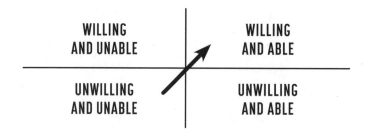

There is one and only one way to scale sales growth effectively on the organizational level, and that is to scale growth on the individual level.

That means the salespeople you hire and retain should be personally oriented toward growth, development, and achievement as their natural state of play. They should have a success trajectory.

They should not need you, or anyone else, to convince them that their best path is up and to the right. To the contrary, up and to the right should already be their instinctive direction. The salespeople you recruit, onboard, and retain should never even be tempted to rest on their laurels. They should walk in the door focused on making the very most of their own potential. Of course, this idea applies not only to salespeople, but to everyone in the organization. (By the way, if you are familiar with the Gartner Group's Magic Quadrant, you already understand this core principle.)

So here's a thought to take forward: Success on both the individual and the team level depends on an up-and-to-the-right movement, a success trajectory, not just on a single project or engagement, not just on a single day, but over the long term. The salespeople who consistently exhibit that success trajectory, not the glossy product photos that show up on your website, are your true product as a sales leader.

Consider: Most business leaders want their products to get better and better over time. They want the service that they deliver to their customers to get better and better over time. They want their organization's innovation to improve over time. They want customer satisfaction to improve over time. But, for some reason, they don't expect the members of their sales team to get better and better over time. There's a disconnect there. This kind of disconnect keeps you from creating what we call the *scalable sales team*. You'll learn more about that kind of team in the next chapter.

Key Takeaways

- There is one and only one way to scale sales growth effectively on the organizational level, and that is to scale growth on the individual level.
- Success on both the individual and the team level depends on an up-and-to-the-right movement, a success trajectory, not just on a single project, not just on a single day, but over the long term.

CHAPTER FOUR

The Scalable Sales Team

RAPID REVENUE GROWTH REQUIRES a scalable organization—and that means first building a productive, scalable sales team.

Here's another way of saying that: Your sales team must be the best-run department in your company. Why? Because revenues drive everything, and the sales team drives revenue. If you want scalable growth, you need a sales team that is producing optimally and is scalable. Most sales teams we encounter aren't producing optimally and aren't scalable. All that means is that the sales leader needs to start thinking differently and behaving differently.

Reality check: If your sales team isn't moving up and to the right and isn't scalable, you are not going to consistently achieve that aggressive revenue objective you've set for your organization. There are two reasons for this. First, your sales team won't be mobilized and

17

headed in a single direction, even if you think it is; and second, your organization as a whole won't be following the sales team's lead. It is important to follow the sales team's lead for the simple reason that the sales team is typically closest to reality as defined by the customer.

When an organization doesn't consistently hit its revenue goals, that means it is stagnating as an organization and has moved away from reality as its customer defines it. You don't have to settle for stagnation if you have the management courage necessary to take action to consciously design the sales team and its support team. This book shows you the specific actions to take. These actions will work for you if:

- You are willing to assume personal responsibility for the results of the sales organization you lead.
- You have the authority to replace staff members.
- You are looking for a better way to sustainably grow the sales organization, and thus the entire business.
- You know that doing what you've always done isn't going to get you where you need to go.
- You are willing to move outside of your comfort zone.

If those bullet points describe you, congratulations. You're in the right place. If you're someone who supports the person we just described, either as a colleague or as a leader—a CEO, board member, investor, or some other interested constituent—we believe what follows will definitely be of interest to you. You will need to know exactly what this person is responsible for executing in order to make aggressive, sustainable growth a reality in your organization.

There is a clear process for delivering that kind of growth and transforming the entire organization. That process starts with the leader of the sales team.

The Devine Group has identified four primary selling models, outlined briefly below.

1. Unique Value Sales

- Demand creation and shorter sales cycle.
- Strong ability to control the sales cycle.
- Moderate to high prospecting requirement.
- Ability to uncover pain and sell pain-based value.

2. Consultative Sales

- Demand creation and longer sales cycle.
- Strong ability to organize and close a long sales process.
- Low to moderate prospecting requirement.
- Ability to uncover pain and sell pain-based value.

3. Account Sales

- Demand fulfillment and longer sales cycle.
- Ability to identify and sell additional business to client.
- Low prospecting requirement.
- Ability to effectively manage client/personal relationships.

4. Commodity Sales

- Demand fulfillment and shorter sales cycle.
- Strong ability to control the sales cycle.

- Moderate to high prospecting requirement.
- Ability to quickly bond with prospects.

The Success Cadence can accelerate revenue growth in all four.

Key Takeaway

- There is a clear process for delivering aggressive, sustainable growth. While there are powerful constituencies and strong opinions in the C-suite, the sales leader (who may go by titles such as: chief revenue officer, vice president of sales, or senior vice president of field operations) is the person best positioned to drive it.

CHAPTER FIVE

The Success Cadence

AS WE'VE SAID, THE RAPID, sustainable growth process we are talking about is called the Success Cadence.

A cadence is a predetermined rhythm. It is constant. It is always playing, always driving you forward, kind of like background music. The first time you try to implement the leadership style we're talking about, it is likely to feel less like background music and more like music that's unfamiliar and distracting. But if you keep at it, you'll find that the rhythm eventually becomes second nature to you and that it gets you into a welcome and productive flow. You may even find that it becomes a part of who you are.

This concept of creating a daily, weekly, quarterly, and annual rhythm for yourself and your team, regardless of your company's size—a rhythm that develops and scales an optimally performing sales force—can transform your organization. But there's a catch: In order for it to work, the leader of the sales team has to be willing to move outside of what is familiar, what has always been sufficient in the past, and what has always been comfortable.

To be wildly successful on the level we're talking about, the sales leader needs to have skin in the game—they must be willing to take a stand and perhaps even put their career at risk. But what is the alternative? Yielding the fast lane to someone else? Consider that your competition may be moving beyond what is comfortable and implementing the same cutting-edge ideas we will be sharing with you—right now, as you're reading these words. If you are a sales leader who is personally committed to getting your team ahead of the pack and keeping it there, to being innovative, to taking intelligent risks and reaping the rewards, this book will show you how.

> *"You never change your life until you step out of your comfort zone; change begins at the end of your comfort zone."*
>
> **–ROY T. BENNETT, AMERICAN AUTHOR**

Product ≠ Success

Rapid growth is only possible if you are willing to move yourself and your team out of a product-driven culture and into a sales-driven culture, one that is focused on the acquisition and retention of willing-and-able people on the sales team. Don't get us wrong. We love product people. But we know from experience that someone who is moving up and to the right in the sales role is, by definition, moving themselves and everyone in the organization (including, for example, product teams) outside of their personal comfort zone, and that this is the key to rapid organizational growth. So we're starting with sales.

> According to smallbiztrends.com, the four-year failure rate for startup companies stands at 44%. Major contributing factors of failure include not assembling the right team, cash flow problems, and (this is important) investing critical resources into developing a product for which there is no market need.

Again: A great product, on its own, is no guarantee of success. There are plenty of underperforming companies with great products and lousy processes—processes that don't support scalable revenue growth.

Our job in this book is to make sure your company isn't one of them. We want to do that by helping you to instill a culture that keeps you close to the market and the customer, a culture that moves all the people on your sales team (including you) up and to the right—and outside of your present comfort zone—as a way of life.

You don't have to be a tech company like Splunk to create a Success Cadence that will unleash your organization's rapid growth culture. As long as you have happy customers and a viable, flexible strategy for keeping them happy, you will find the Success Cadence growth process to be effective, intuitive, adaptable to the unique history and market environment of your company, and (perhaps most important) scalable.

The Success Cadence is all about today. It's a way of running your team and your business that instantly differentiates you, that distinguishes good from great, that allows small companies to grow at a rapid rate (if that's what they want to do and are willing to invest in), and to improve aggressively across the board. Anyone in your industry who applies the Success Cadence principles and runs their business accordingly has a strategic advantage. Conversely, companies that do not apply these principles run the very real risk of falling behind. We believe the Success Cadence is not optional if you are in business to be successful; it's a requirement to compete in today's economy.

Key Takeaway

- By implementing the Success Cadence growth process, you can make aggressive, sustainable growth a reality on your sales team and for your entire organization—if you are willing to move yourself, your team, and your entire company out of existing comfort zones.

CHAPTER SIX

The Challenge

THE PROCESS WE WILL BE sharing with you here will only work if you take it as a personal challenge.

It will be a personal challenge to you because it requires that you take a radically different approach to recruiting, training, coaching, and developing teams—and then stick with that process. This is not the flavor of the month. This is a plan for launching and sustaining an organizational growth trajectory based on sound operational data and a clear commitment to the personal growth trajectory of every salesperson who reports to you.

Specifically, the Success Cadence process requires a culture-driven, talent-driven, data-driven approach to leadership that most leaders, in our experience, are simply not used to and won't commit to. This new type of leadership means you accept personal responsibility for protecting the positive working culture of the team and for putting the right people in the right positions—not just today, not just tomorrow, but constantly looking forward to the next 6 to 18 months. It means accepting personal responsibility to identify, onboard, coach, and retain high-potential contributors—people who can make a dramatic positive impact now and perhaps an even more dramatic positive impact a year or so down the line. These people may be even better than you are! What greater accomplishment could you ask for, given that you are personally responsible for whatever those people accomplish?

This style of leadership requires a different set of processes, a different approach to measurement, and a different set of assumptions than you may be used to. It also requires the willingness and ability to go outside your current comfort zone. It requires what we call *management courage*—the willingness to actually do what you know you ought to do, but for whatever reason have put off doing.

Consider: Most leaders we talk to say that they really are committed to identifying and holding onto the people whose metrics clearly identify them as high-potential contributors. Then we look at their turnover figures, and we realize a huge number of those high-potential hires leave the company before they can make a meaningful contribution—and a huge number of underperformers remain on staff. The leaders are doing nothing to change this state of affairs. It's become part of their company DNA.

This means their process isn't working. They need to change that process. Taking action to make that change is, we submit, a management courage moment.

You may be experiencing such a moment right now. It's all too easy for leaders to rationalize this outcome as being something other than their issue. "If the compensation package were different, our retention numbers would be better..." "If millennials were more loyal, our retention numbers would be better..." And so on.

Is any of this ringing a bell? If so, please consider the following possibilities.

- Those employees didn't leave because they were millennials.
- They didn't leave because they were inherently disloyal.
- They didn't leave because they were out to make a quick buck somewhere else.
- They came to you for a reason, but they left because you didn't have the right process in place for hiring, training, and motivating a team in which the right salespeople wanted to work—and stick around—even if they were being paid less than the competition offered at the starting level.

In essence, you didn't set them up for success.

There is a process for making that happen. You don't have it yet. We're emphasizing this uncomfortable truth because you need to accept it before we move on—and because senior leadership too often leaves people in sales to their own devices, failing to supply a process or any meaningful support or guidance. Standards must be set. People must be led. A process must be in place. These are the essential requirements for delivering value in a scalable way. If there is a pattern of good people leaving you, that means you haven't set the standards, led the people, or implemented the process.

If you don't believe you had something to do with the current environment and culture you have created, then we can't help you. On the other hand, if you are willing to accept that you can change the status quo and the culture because you created it—if you are willing to challenge, revisit, and redefine your own responsibilities as a leader—then we can do business.

> *"Culture is manifested in the way people behave*
> *when they are unsure and afraid."*
>
> **—COREY THOMAS, CEO, RAPID7**

In today's economy, a scorched-earth approach to talent acquisition and retention is simply not sustainable. Word gets around. Your organization is either a destination employer where people are eager to build a career, or it isn't. Right now, the fact that you're reading this book tells us that it probably isn't.

Please keep reading only if you are willing to make changes in the areas where we ask you to take action. Please consider the decision to make that commitment, and continue with this book, your first management courage moment.

Key Takeaway

- The Success Cadence is a proven process for scaling your team. But, in order to implement that process, you will need to be ready to move outside your comfort zone. That means regularly challenging, revisiting, and redefining your own responsibilities as a leader.

CHAPTER SEVEN

The Art and Skill of Momentum

CREATING A REPEATABLE, INCREASING, SCALABLE rhythm of measurable, strategically sound activity is a momentum revolution. This revolution starts within the sales team and eventually encompasses the organization as a whole. By implementing the concepts and strategies you will encounter here, you will be able to set aggressive but realistic revenue goals at the strategic level—and then create the layered teams, systems, and tactics that make forward momentum not only possible on those revenue goals, but part of your organization's identity.

There is both an art and a skill to establishing and maintaining that momentum. The problem is, activity for the sake of activity usually takes precedence. This doesn't happen when you follow the

Success Cadence. We will show you how to create momentum based on activity that actually generates revenue—and we'll show how to get better at putting out the inevitable fires that flare up.

The Success Cadence has the power to create rapid, sustainable, aggressive growth—growth that is driven by the internal momentum necessary to crush your competitors and transform your organization's culture in the process. In fact, in our experience, it's impossible to grow rapidly and sustain that growth without transforming the culture.

This next part surprises a lot of people.

Used properly, the Success Cadence will win you time. When you think of your business now, it's likely that you think about how you're always scrambling for time. What if you found more of it? What if you and your team could punch above your weight, get more done in less time, and still have time to go to your child's recital or coach the soccer team?

The Success Cadence is marketplace rocket fuel, waiting to be ignited. It just needs your commitment to follow through—your management courage to do what it takes to turn your organization into a destination employer for high-potential contributors—starting with those who can have an immediate positive impact on the performance of the sales team. There really is a rhythm for doing this, a clear sequence of steps and an organizational cadence that your sales team can establish in order to move from where you are now to where you want to be. We will show you how to set and sustain that rhythm. You begin by looking closely at the culture of your team.

Your first and essential order of business is to launch and sustain a rapid-growth culture throughout your sales organization, with you as the leader and primary exemplar of that culture.

Supporting a rapid-growth culture with your own personal example means identifying and changing familiar processes that have been in place for a while but aren't working.

Supporting a rapid-growth culture with your own personal example isn't always going to be easy, and it isn't always going to be comfortable. It will, however, be something you can get better at over time and can update consistently based on real-world information so that you can see the results—and become more and more confident as you go forward that you really are making the right call.

What you are holding in your hands—this book—is basically a blueprint for a revolution from within, one that takes consistent, concerted, persistent effort over time in order to succeed, not just within the sales team, but throughout the entire organization. Like all revolutions, this one will eventually lead you to step on some toes. Like all revolutions, the Success Cadence will, at some point, take other people, not just you, out of the comfort zone. Like all revolutions, it will not be universally popular.

But the revolution is worth leading anyway.

"Building a sales machine is a blend of science and art. You need lots of data, lots of measurement of the right things, combined with experiential aspects that are continually refined and added into the mix. There is no one big thing. It is a lot of little things coming together every day. Ongoing refinement is very important."

–RAJESH RAM, CO-FOUNDER AND CHIEF CUSTOMER OFFICER, EGNYTE

Key Takeaways

- The Success Cadence is a repeatable, increasing, scalable rhythm of measurable, strategically sound activity, starting with the sales team and spreading outward from there.

- Supporting a rapid-growth culture with your own personal example means identifying and changing familiar processes that have been in place for a while but aren't working.

- Supporting a rapid-growth culture with your own personal example isn't always going to be easy, and it isn't always going to be comfortable.

- As long as you have happy customers and a product or service capable of keeping them happy, rapid growth is achievable—regardless of where your company is right now in its growth cycle and regardless of what industry you operate in.

CHAPTER EIGHT

Changing How You Lead

WE'VE FOUND THAT SUCCESSFUL IMPLEMENTATION of the Success Cadence throughout an organization depends on the behavior, attitude, and skills of everyone on the sales team, especially those of the sales leader. To set the right culture, you must lead. You must be congruent—that is, you must practice exactly what you preach. You must be willing to challenge the status quo as you go forward.

The first and most important challenge lies in understanding your own job description. To restate, your job is to find and hold onto salespeople who are both willing and able. That's what makes rapid growth possible. You cannot delegate this job. All you can do is empower others to align with and defend the culture you develop as you take on the mission of aggressively growing the sales team.

There will be distractions. It will be tempting to move on to other important matters, and sometimes you will need to. But as the sales leader, you are still the only person who is personally responsible for making time to understand and follow through on the cultural revolution implicit in the deceptively simple-sounding words "willing" and "able"—a revolution that starts within you and moves steadily outward over time.

The Success Cadence revolution always starts within the leader of a sales team, large or small; it is always launched, modeled, promoted and defended by you, in close collaboration with the senior leadership of your company; and it always expands outward. In this revolution, the sales organization's operating cadence eventually sets the rhythm for every other team in the organization, whether or not that team is responsible for sales. That operating rhythm challenges some core assumptions about who should be calling the shots, which is as it should be. Why? Because salespeople and company leaders are entrepreneurial in nature—and entrepreneurs with discipline are key enablers and promoters in rapid-growth organizations.

Implementing the Success Cadence means that instead of operating with an operational hierarchy like this:

Traditional Slow-Moving Companies

Corporate finance drives:

- Product development
- Product management
- Operations
- Marketing
- Sales

... you're actually responsible for creating and operating within an operational hierarchy that looks more like this:

Success Cadence Companies

Executive committee (which includes the sales leader) drives:

- Sales, which drives:
  - Corporate finance
  - Product development
  - Product management
  - Operations
  - Marketing

Make no mistake. The rest of the organization must follow the rhythm, the cadence, that you, the sales leader, establish as you carry out your responsibility to attract, onboard, support, and retain an escalating, but always targeted, number of salespeople who are both willing and able. Sustaining that rhythm, no matter what, is your job. If you didn't know that was your job, now you do. In carrying out that job, you will need to drive budgeting decisions. By the way, the relationship between sales and finance, at least in the beginning, is absolutely critical—and far more important, at least in the beginning, than the relationship between, say, sales and marketing.

What we have outlined is an untraditional model, one that upsets some people's assumptions (maybe yours). But it's the only model that delivers aggressive growth.

Remember: Making all of this happen means launching an organizational revolution. You will need the support of the CEO, founder, or president of your company if this revolution is to succeed. Be sure to share this book with them. As you do so, be sure to tell them:

"What really happens when sales is at the back end of the organizational chart? What are the real-world implications of that choice? Here's the answer. Someone else decides on the product, the marketing, the number that need to be sold and the compensation program—and then the sales team is informed that it needs to step up and sell it. This is a hit-or-miss proposition at best, and very often the emphasis is on 'miss.' Why? Because sometimes the sales team—the team that is by definition closest to the customer base—is introduced into the game too late to make a difference."

The Success Cadence lays out a radically different plan of attack. In this model, the executive committee—typically the CEO/founder and the lead finance person—sets the strategic direction of the company in collaboration with you, the sales leader. You share that strategic direction with your team, which you are personally responsible for recruiting, retaining, and growing, and then you lead that team in creating the action plan. You work with them to get absolute clarity on who they need to target, what territories they will focus on, what resources are needed to succeed, and how you can best support them. Then the rest of the organization can follow your lead and support the sales team as it succeeds—and expands. This is what rapid growth looks like. If you follow the Success Cadence, steady action in support of expanding revenue and expanding the company's success in the marketplace becomes the heartbeat of the entire organization.

This discussion requires courage, because CEOs and founders often carry a persona of untouchability. Many organizations reach growth plateaus because the CEO/founder chooses to indulge that persona at the expense of building a scalable organization. However, those who are coachable, those who surround themselves with people who have experience beyond their personal scope, are those who succeed at the highest level. Someone bold may have to step up and help the CEO/founder of your organization to see this if the organization's growth trajectory is to change. That bold person is you.

"Stop wearing your wishbone where your backbone ought to be."
–ELIZABETH GILBERT, AMERICAN AUTHOR

It is key that you, yourself, set up this system of collaboration with and accountability to the executive committee. Regular updates from you and strategy sessions with you will build your critical credibility with these key players. You are willing to involve them, to share your plans and goals with them before sharing them with anyone else, and to be measured on attaining those goals, officially and publicly. In return, you'll find they will bend over backwards to help you—you just have to make the first move.

"One of the most important topics is creating balance and constructive tension between the sales leader and the CFO. How do you align company objectives with giving the growth engine time to scale? How do you invest in the right places? Salespeople talk to each other. Compensation plans that are sales-friendly (and hence might at first appear CFO-unfriendly) are essential to establishing a culture where salespeople feel they can make money. That's important, because a few winning salespeople can attract many more winning ones. That's how the engine feeds itself."

–RAJESH RAM, CO-FOUNDER AND CHIEF CUSTOMER OFFICER, EGNYTE

Key Takeaways

- When you follow the Success Cadence, the sales organization's operating rhythm eventually sets the rhythm for every other team in the organization, whether or not that team is responsible for sales.
- Making that happen means launching an organizational revolution. You will need the support of the CEO, founder, or president of your company and that of the lead finance person if this revolution is to succeed. Be sure to share and discuss this book with them.

CHAPTER NINE

Changing How You Recruit

ANOTHER CORE ASSUMPTION THAT NEEDS to change (if you are taking the Success Cadence journey) has to do with how salespeople are selected in the first place. Effective sales leaders focus intensely on the goal of selecting the right people.

Many sales leaders we work with have a set of core assumptions that leads them to select the wrong salespeople for the team. They hire and work hard to retain salespeople who have what we call a *me-first* attitude. That's counterproductive to rapid growth.

Imagine you were responsible for the performance of a sports team, such as a football, hockey, soccer, or basketball team. Wouldn't you want people on your team who didn't argue with you about when they were rotated in or out? People who executed the plays you'd designed in such a way that the team scored, regardless of their personal statistics? Of course, you would—and not just because working with selfish players can be exhausting. When there is a me-first working culture, the team doesn't perform at anything close to its full potential.

What's true for a sports team is just as true for your sales team. When there is an me-first culture, the team as a whole can't establish a viable operating rhythm. People are always stopping what they're doing to deal with some kind of needless drama. It could be drama involving another salesperson, or drama involving a team in a different part of the organization, or drama involving someone on the internal support team—but there is always some kind of soap opera going on when the culture is not consistently what we call *we-first*. As a result, the company misses out on huge opportunities, day after day after day.

A me-first attitude from even one person on your team directly conflicts with the requirements of a rapid-growth culture, regardless of the size of your team or your company. Not noticing that reality and not acting on it is a key characteristic of underperforming sales leaders.

It's important to note here that we're not in the business of stifling creativity or innovation. But we do believe there's a clear dividing line between creativity and a me-first culture. Creativity that supports group objectives and mutual agreements is a powerful, distinguishing competitive force; but unstable, random "going it alone" creativity that polarizes workforces, creates rivalries, and keeps teams from working a shared sales process together is toxic and unscalable. It kills companies. If this "creativity" is valued at the expense of team-wide calendar discipline, collaboration, commitment to clearly stated critical goals, and mutual respect, then it's not really creativity. It's a downward spiral.

Because we don't want you to have to deal with that downward spiral, we want to help you challenge your own core assumptions about what a good sales hire looks like. In order to do that, we have to tell you a story. This particular story happens to be true. Whether or not you're familiar with it, it's quite important that you read this story closely and that you consider its implications for sales leaders, which are far-reaching. We'll make this part of the book easier by giving you the moral of this story ahead of time. Here it is:

> "If everyone is moving forward together, then success takes care of itself" (Henry Ford, founder, Ford Motor Company).

And now, here's the story. Note that it has nothing to do with Henry Ford—beyond agreeing with him that a we-first outlook is what produces good outcomes.

The Miracle

Once upon a time, a man named Herb Brooks decided to recruit for the U.S. Olympic hockey team in an unorthodox manner.

You may have heard of Brooks. (He's the subject of a wonderful movie called *Miracle*.) Whether you've heard of him or not, what you need to know about him is this: Brooks focused heavily on the cohesion of the team he was assembling—on its ability to perform as a team in specific situations.

He did not focus as much as other hockey coaches did on individual performance statistics. He did not pick the players that any number of experts would have chosen as the top players in the country on the assumption that those players would somehow find a way to work well together.

Here are some of the other remarkable things Herb Brooks did do in putting America's 1980 Olympic hockey team together.

- He focused heavily on players he knew of through his own network.
- He committed himself and his team to a carefully designed training regimen meant to prepare them for all the work that lay ahead.
- He conducted personality assessments (today, these instruments are called "psychometric assessments") to identify the players likeliest to respond best to his coaching style and to the requirements of the team.
- He built a template for the ideal player for his team, one that included both ability attributes (specific skills or talent connected to the position in question) and willingness attributes (for instance: open to being coached, creative, capable of responding well in high-stress situations). Brooks called the attributes that went beyond skill or talent the player's *value system.*
- The 68 players he allowed to try out for his team were carefully evaluated both for their skills and for their value system (what we call *willingness* in this book).
- He got rid of players who did not show the necessary willingness attributes, regardless of their ability attributes.

By following this plan, Brooks assembled the youngest, least experienced team in U.S. hockey history. He also challenged all the conventional coaching wisdom in amateur American hockey up to that point.

Having assembled a team that left some experts shaking their heads, Brooks proceeded to rewrite the existing U.S. Olympic preparation process, demanding a grueling 61-game schedule that required massive amounts of training time from his young players. He exposed them to a wide range of international opponents, and he built up their physical endurance. Brooks was out to develop a process that would create, in the words of hockey historian Wayne Coffey, "the most fit team in the world."

Even so, the reality was that the group Brooks assembled in 1979 and took into the Olympic Games in 1980 was significantly younger and had significantly less international playing time than the team that was heavily favored to win the gold medal that year: the Russians. As a result, none of the experts expected much from the Americans.

Brooks's team was, however, composed of players who were both willing and able to do their jobs. By the time the Olympics started, those players had established a shared team rhythm on the ice—and they were in the best shape of their lives. Brooks's team was composed entirely of players who thought about we-first before they thought about me-first. Brooks's team was composed entirely of players that had been coached, prepared, and relentlessly conditioned by Brooks to function as a team in key aspects of the game.

In the end, that hockey team pulled off what has since come to be known as the "Miracle on Ice." They did what no one but Herb Brooks and his team believed was possible: They destroyed a much more experienced, much better resourced competitor. They beat the Russians—and they went on to win the gold medal.

Our question for you is: How?

1. Consider the possibility that Herb Brooks understood that his true product was hockey players who were both willing and able to do the job he had defined, with the emphasis on willing. Think of your own experience as a manager. You can usually bring people up to speed on being able if you need to—but you typically can't budge the "willing" indicator. If someone isn't willing, then you cannot expect to bring them up to the right level of ability. The two go hand-in-hand.

2. Consider that one particularly important aspect of a player's being willing to do the job Brooks had defined was attitudinal. His players had to have a we-first mentality, as opposed to a me-first mentality. Think of your own sales team. Do any of them ever expect to play by rules that are different than the rules others have to follow?

3. Consider that Brooks developed a system that ensured that his team members were far better conditioned than the competition. He implemented that process at the very beginning of the players' journey with him. Think of your own onboarding process for salespeople. Is it clear? Is it systematized? Is it written down? Does it create (and support) team members who are willing and able, who work as a team, and who are playing at the top of their game?

"Great salespeople are like athletes at the top of their game; like great athletes, they practice the fundamentals relentlessly, role-play critical situations, and get coaching to improve every aspect of their game."

—BRIAN SULLIVAN, AMERICAN AUTHOR AND BUSINESS EXECUTIVE;
VICE PRESIDENT, SANDLER ENTERPRISE SELLING

Key Takeaways

- Me-first has no place in your organization.
- Herb Brooks focused on a recruiting strategy that had a heavy team focus, not a me-first focus. You can, too.
- Willingness and ability are the key attributes of successful members of your sales team, and willingness must lead the way. One of the critical willingness values is the ability to think about we-first outcomes before thinking about me-first outcomes.
- Most sales leaders don't screen or hire for a we-first rather than me-first outlook. If you're going to do your job of finding and holding onto willing and able salespeople, you must.
- Designing, creating, and defending a willingness and ability culture—a we-first culture—is one of your critical responsibilities as a leader.

CHAPTER TEN

Your Willing-and-Able Matrix

IT'S TIME TO GET TO WORK. On a separate sheet of paper, draw a cross of two axes, with the up-and-down axis marked "willing" and the left-to-right axis marked "able." Do this right now.

You should now be looking at a piece of paper with a simple design that looks very much like the image you see on the next page.

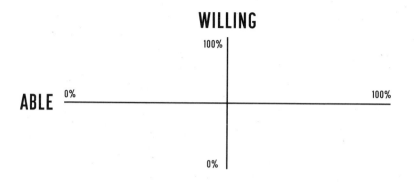

Are you with us so far? If you're looking at a sheet of paper that shows what you see above, drawn very large, we're going to assume the answer is "yes."

Here's the next question: Do you want a sales team, and eventually an entire organization, with a heavy team focus, one that consists entirely of people who are both willing and able to play as an ensemble, at the very top of their game? If your answer here is "yes" (and it should be!), you will need to become familiar with what is happening in each of the four quadrants of the willing-and-able matrix. You should now label the four blanks of what you've drawn so that it looks like this:

WILLING

100%

WILLING AND UNABLE	WILLING AND ABLE

ABLE 0% ———————————————— 100%

UNWILLING AND UNABLE	UNWILLING AND ABLE

0%

Have you done that? Great. Now, within each of those four spaces, write down the name of one specific salesperson who either works for you now or who worked with you for at least 90 days before moving on (for whatever reason).

In other words:

- In the upper-right quadrant, write the name of a real salesperson you believe was both highly willing and clearly able to do the job, however you define the job of salesperson right now. It's likely, but not mandatory, that this is one of your top contributors.
  - This is the person on your team who wants to succeed and takes action on that desire.
  - This person consistently does what it takes to get the job done.
  - This person has the capability to perform the tasks necessary to consistently complete a successful sales cycle at a very high level.
  - This person has a we-first mindset, not a me-first mindset.
  - This person does not expect special treatment.
  - This person is motivated by the job and the reward. You don't have to motivate them separately.

Broadly speaking, this person has both the skills and experience to succeed. They are already proficient in the key areas needed to do a great job.

Important: Proof that the person is able to do the job must be demonstrated in performance metrics, not in promises or forecasts.

Equally important: If a person you are considering for this quadrant has even once displayed the attitude of "the rules everyone else plays by don't apply to me," please pick someone else you feel is both willing and able to do the job of salesperson in your organization.

Equally, equally important: Note that this quadrant is reserved for self-starters. If this person constantly needs you to provide motivation, please pick someone else you feel is both willing and able to fulfill the job of salesperson in your organization.

- In the upper-left quadrant, write the name of a real salesperson you believe is willing to do the job, but not yet able to do so at a high level (or at all). For instance, this might be a highly motivated, enthusiastic recent hire who has not yet learned the ropes about your methodology, process, tools, product, or service.

  - The willing and unable person is the one who puts the work in, who wants to succeed, and who is committed to executing the behaviors that are necessary to achieve success, but for some reason there are some gaps in their skills profile. This person doesn't have the experience in some areas that they need to be successful.

  - This could be the result of a lack of training in a critical area, or it could be the result of poor execution of the skills that haven't yet been reinforced to the point where they are owned. Note that the team's sales leader (the front line manager in most cases) has the prime responsibility of identifying, coaching, and determining whether the person will eventually be capable—and will ultimately be held accountable for the individual's performance.

  - It's therefore the sales leader's job to find out why the person is unable and what will bring them into the "able" category.

- In the lower-right quadrant, write the name of a real salesperson you believe is able to do the job, but is not currently willing to do so, for whatever reason. For instance, this could be someone who was once a peak performer, but who has been coasting for a while and whose revenue totals reflect that. Alternatively, they may not understand the company culture or they may not embrace the reality that you place a high value on learning, agility, teamwork, and calendar discipline.

- The able but unwilling team member is the person on your team who isn't working to their potential for some reason.

- Such team members may simply be unwilling to move beyond their current comfort zone and take the actions necessary to move their careers to the next level.

- Alternatively, they may be facing a personal situation, such as a health issue or a major relationship or family problem, which is causing them to hold back from taking action to do what needs to be done in order to succeed.

- Finally, in the lower-left quadrant, write the name of a real salesperson you believe is (or was) both unwilling and unable to sell effectively for your team. This could be someone who simply did not want to commit to the role of salesperson, or who had a basic skill gap that couldn't or didn't get closed.

  - This could be someone who is not now posting and has never posted the kind of metrics that indicate that it is possible for them to succeed within the role of salesperson. (A side note: If you don't yet know what measurable performance indicators demonstrate the capacity to succeed within the role of salesperson, that is part of the gap you will need to close as a sales leader. As you will see, it is easy to set up trackable, measurable performance metrics for each person on your team.)

- This could be a new hire that was made without due diligence on your part. If you've ever made a bad hire for your sales team (and you're certainly not alone if you have), then it should be fairly easy for you to think of this name.

- The person whose name you write in this quadrant could also be someone who has just been moved into a new position that they did not want. A veteran salesperson who has been moved into a very different role than the one they are familiar with and happy performing is a classic example of someone in the "unwilling and unable" quadrant.

- If a person is consistently unwilling and unable to perform the role in question, then it's time to make a change.

Of course, these assessments are private. They are meant for your eyes only and for the people you report to. If you want to build trust in the organization and reap the massive benefits of that organizational value, it goes without saying that you will keep this sensitive sheet of paper to yourself.

(A side note: Ideally, you would conduct the same exercise for field support people who work with your sales team. At the very least, however, you should become familiar with how the willing-and-able matrix works for the members of the sales staff.)

"If you pick the right people and give them the opportunity to spread their wings and put compensation as a carrier behind it, you almost don't have to manage them."

–JACK WELCH, AMERICAN BUSINESS LEADER

Key Takeaway

- The four quadrants of your willing-and-able matrix break down as follows: "willing and able"; "willing and unable"; "unwilling and able"; "unwilling and unable."
- Write down the names of actual salespeople from your world who match these criteria. Keep the sheet to yourself. Don't show your sheet to anyone. Don't move on to the next chapter until you have done this.

CHAPTER ELEVEN

A Deeper Dive on the Willing-and-Able Matrix

AFTER THE EXERCISE IN THE prior chapter, you should now be looking at a box divided into four quadrants. Each quadrant should contain the name of one actual salesperson from your world who fits the criteria for that box.

Specifically, you should be looking at the name of someone who is willing and able in the upper-right quadrant. Later on in the book, we'll talk about the other three names you've written on this sheet. For right now, let's focus on your willing and able person.

This individual represents your ideal sales hire—not so much because of where they are now, but because of the direction you feel they are headed.

You want to hire and retain only people who are headed in this up-and-to-the-right direction. Doing an in-depth willing-and-able analysis of someone on your team is a matter of generating a data-driven snapshot of where that person is at this moment. It will not necessarily show you where they are headed next month, next quarter, or next year. Your job is to accumulate multiple data points over time, so that the direction becomes clearer. Where you feel the person is headed and what data makes you feel that way should eventually be part of your one-on-one discussions with this individual.

Remember what we have established about your job description: Salespeople who are both willing and able to do their job are your real product, which you as the sales leader are responsible for delivering. That means you want to attract, motivate, and retain people who are consistently headed in the up-and-to-the-right direction.

We are repeating this point because it is central to the implementation of the Success Cadence in your organization. If what you just read doesn't make sense in your world, if it doesn't become a personal priority for you as a sales leader, the rest of this book will be of little or no use to you. So, forgive us if we take this opportunity to emphasize the point: The person you put in the upper-right quadrant of that sheet is proof that you have, at some point, done your job. This is the direction in which the entire team must go.

Up and to the right is the true north of your compass, both for yourself as an individual and for your team. It is the cultural norm you must recruit, coach to, and reward. The goal of moving up and to the right is the DNA, the foundation, and the guiding idea behind literally everything you do. It's your cultural and personal guiding star. Please take this opportunity to look at the matrix once again and notice where you show up.

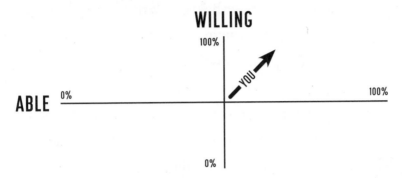

Again: That arrow is the success trajectory. Your job as a sales leader is not only to make success trajectory hires, but also to live and model the success trajectory.

Right now, your own challenge is to live the success trajectory by sharing what you've learned so far with your top leadership. Here's how you're going to do that.

Before you move on to Chapter 12, schedule and hold an informal conversation with someone from the senior leadership of your organization (or as high as you can get within it). Have a frank and confidential discussion about what you've learned so far about those four names on your sheet.

Explain, in private, to this senior leadership person (ideally, the president, CEO, or founder) how important it is to you personally to grow the revenue in the sales team. Explain that you need help and support in doing that, and share your ideas for creating a rapid-growth sales culture, given what you've learned here so far.

Specifically, explain the willing-and-able model, as it relates to your future sales hires and your present staffing decisions.

During this meeting, acknowledge openly that not everyone who wants a job or wants to keep a job on your sales team is now represented by that up-and-to-the-right arrow. By the way, this is entirely natural. Every company will require some unique skills that must be taught and reinforced. Most salespeople don't walk in the door both willing and able. Most salespeople seek to join a company knowing they must have a willingness to learn or they won't even get the job offer. As a result, sales hires typically walk in the door with high willingness and low ability, relative to the key skills that are required for success in the position. Some of them reach a point where they sustain a success trajectory—some don't. If you aren't comfortable discussing this fact with senior leadership, become comfortable with it. If your team as a whole is not on a success trajectory right now, acknowledge that.

A side observation: This is all about attracting A-level talent. Companies that don't invest heavily in the proper skills training, tooling, process development, coaching, and overall culture will always attract B-level talent. Talent follows talent. The very best people want to work with the best, and they want to be associated with success. They want to work in a place they believe will make them successful. If companies don't believe and invest in A-level talent, they fall behind.

During your meeting with this senior leadership person, accept personal responsibility for ensuring that everyone you hire and retain from this point forward not only learns the core skills, but also maintains a clear up-and-to-right performance track—a success trajectory. State directly during this meeting that salespeople who don't maintain that path—either due to performance issues or due to a company-culture mismatch—don't belong, and can't stay, on your team. Commit to this senior leadership person that you will be reporting back on a monthly basis on how you're doing with coaching, supporting, and eventually reassigning or parting company with the people who don't give you measurable evidence of being able to reach, attain, and sustain that success trajectory.

It may help to loan this senior leadership person a copy of this book. That's entirely up to you. However you choose to do it, schedule and hold this meeting before you move on to the next chapter. This is incredibly important, because initiating and sustaining the Success Cadence is impossible without discussions involving close collaboration and clear commitments between the sales leader and the executive team.

Here's another interesting exercise you and your CEO can do. Privately list your direct reports in no particular order. Now ask yourself: If this were your company, your P&L, and your money funding the salaries and overhead, would you have hired or would you now keep all of those people on your list? Put a "Y" next to those you would keep and an "X" next to those you would not. (Again, keep this exercise private.)

By the way—if you happen to be the founder, CEO, or president of your company and you are also the sales leader, that's great. Please make a point of having the same discussion we've just outlined with an accountability partner of your choice (such as your coach or someone in your peer group). Share what you've learned thus far about the willing-and-able matrix and commit to monthly updates about coaching, supporting, and eventually reassigning or parting company with salespeople who don't provide measurable evidence of being able to reach, attain, and sustain a success trajectory.

Key Takeaway

- Initiating and sustaining the Success Cadence is impossible without discussions involving close collaboration and clear commitments between the sales leader and the executive team. Such commitments are the foundation of a sales-oriented, market-driven culture. Without them, you will struggle to make progress.

CHAPTER TWELVE

Your Management Courage Moment

EARLIER IN THIS BOOK, WE asked you to make a personal commitment to act on management courage moments as they arose. The first of these moments, which you passed, was the agreement to keep reading and keep learning, at the end of Chapter 6. Remember? That was pretty easy, right?

From this point on, it gets a little tougher.

Case in point: You, and what's happening right now.

If you are now reading these words without having had a face-to-face or voice-to-voice discussion about what you learned from the willing-and-able matrix exercise with a member of the senior leadership team in your company and without having made a personal commitment to deliver monthly updates to that person, guess what? You have not yet taken action on the second, and the most critical, of your management courage moments.

"Life shrinks or expands in proportion to one's courage."
–ANAIS NIN, AMERICAN-CUBAN-FRENCH ESSAYIST

As you may recall, the only possible exception to this is if you happen to be the founder, president, or CEO of your company, in which case this particular management courage moment required you to have the same conversation with a peer who can serve as your accountability partner and to make the same commitment to monthly updates to that person.

In either case, if you haven't had the discussion and made the commitment, you are currently stuck inside your present comfort zone. You are not in a position to lead or model the Success Cadence.

At the present moment, your personal willing-and-able matrix is stagnant. It is not taking you out of your comfort zone. It is not moving up and to the right. Instead of a success trajectory arrow, it is likely your personal willing-and-able matrix is not an arrow at all, but is a dot. Something like this:

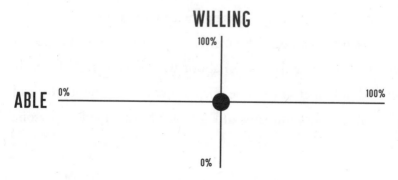

Which is, sad but true, the first step toward this:

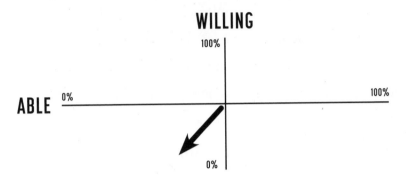

That, of course, is a failure trajectory. Note, too, that, as the company moves up and to the right, a stagnant trajectory quickly becomes a failure trajectory. You have fallen behind by default. That is not where you want to be as the leader of your team, and it's certainly not where you want your team to be.

If you did not take action at the end of Chapter 11, you bought into a failure trajectory. It doesn't make you a bad person or a bad leader—it's just worth noticing, for at least two reasons. Reason 1: Most people don't take action, which is pretty interesting if they want to distinguish themselves from their competition. Reason 2: You not taking action was actually an important learning opportunity for you as a sales leader.

Why? Because the reasons you didn't take action when we asked you to move beyond your comfort zone are the identical reasons members of your team won't take action, at first, when you challenge them to move beyond their comfort zone. (By the way, even if you did take action as we requested at the end of the previous chapter, you should closely consider what follows.)

Full disclosure: Every chapter we share with you from this point forward will feature commitments that you may not feel like implementing at first, but need to implement anyway. The reason you won't feel like implementing them will be your natural human resistance to change. This powerful emotional response to change goes through four stages, which we encourage you now to notice when (not if, when) they play out in your own mind:

1. **Denial: "We don't have that problem."** For instance: "We already do a good job of recruiting and retaining high-potential salespeople." Unfortunately, you don't. If you did, you would be growing faster than you are now.

2. **Resistance (covert or overt): "That wouldn't work here."** For instance: "We've tried something like what you're suggesting before." Or, "Other people have tried something like that before." Obviously, you didn't identify and implement the right approach, because if you had, you'd have a sales team composed exclusively of high-potential salespeople who want to stick around, even though competitors are offering to pay them more. (Yes, that is really what happens on teams that implement the Success Cadence. More on that later.)

3. **Exploration: "Maybe that does make sense."** This is where you think, "Hmm... They may be onto something. They've made it work." Or, "I never thought about it that way. How would I do that here at my company?"

4. **Commitment: "Here's what I am personally responsible for doing differently."** You think: "OK, I will personally commit to this process." Not the team. Not your support staff. You.

This is the courage moment, the moment that takes you out of your comfort zone and up and to the right.

Everyone—and we do mean everyone—who makes moving up and to the right a daily personal reality goes through these four responses to constructive change. You will. Your team will, too.

Key Takeaways

- Everyone goes through four predictable responses to change: denial, resistance, exploration, and commitment.
- That goes for you, and it goes for the members of the sales team you lead.
- Reaching a point of commitment is a courage moment that takes you out of your comfort zone and moves you up and to the right. This is your management courage moment.
- And, as in the prior chapter, initiating and sustaining the Success Cadence is impossible without discussions involving close collaboration and clear commitments between the sales leader and the executive team.

Your Commitment

- If you haven't already done so, commit to having a face-to-face or voice-to-voice discussion about what you learned from the willing-and-able matrix exercise in Chapter 11 with a member of the senior leadership team in your company and to deliver monthly updates to that person on the actions you have taken in support of establishing a Success Cadence. (If you happen to be the founder, CEO, or president of the company, in addition to being the sales leader, revise what you just read so that your commitment is to a peer of your choosing.) Then—follow through!

CHAPTER THIRTEEN

Your Ideal Sales Hire

WELCOME BACK. OUR WORKING ASSUMPTION now is that you have successfully navigated that second management courage moment, which means you have already had at least one voice-to-voice discussion about all this within what we will now call your *executive committee*. At this point you should have a clear understanding of these three things:

1. What your most important responsibility is as a sales leader (namely to find, attract, hire, and retain salespeople who are both willing and able).
2. How the willing-and-able matrix works and, specifically, why you placed the four names on the matrix in the slots that you did.

3. When your next face-to-face or voice-to-voice meeting with your executive committee is. This meeting should be booked in both of your calendars for no later than 30 days from the first time you met. If you want to make it more frequent than that, more power to you.

Assuming that all of that is in place, congratulations are in order. You are officially on a success trajectory. You are moving up and to the right as a sales leader. That's definitely the right direction.

Your challenge now is to get a clearer fix on your ideal sales hire. It is time to get down, on paper, exactly what the ideal sales candidate looks like in your organization. In the next two chapters, we will help you to get the ball rolling on that key deliverable—without which rapid, scalable sales growth is impossible.

In preparation for completing that deliverable, let's revisit a principle that, by now, we're hoping is already very familiar to you: Success on both the individual and the team level depends on up-and-to-the-right movement, not just on a single project, not just on a single day, but for the long term.

You already know that, which means you also already know that moving up and to the right is the core recruiting requirement. Moving up and to the right is the cultural norm you want to identify, retain, and reward. It is the DNA, the foundation, the guiding idea, behind the Success Cadence. Tangible evidence for moving up and to the right needs to drive every one of your staffing decisions.

This cultural and personal ideal, as you'll recall, looks like this when expressed graphically in its simplest form:

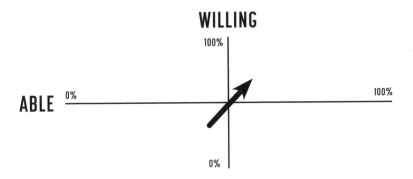

Of course, your job as a sales leader is to make success trajectory hires. We're recapping what you know already because it's so important to what follows.

Something you also know now but may not yet have taken action on is the corollary to all of this, which is that not everyone who wants a job (or wants to keep a job) on your sales team will be represented by that up-and-to-the-right arrow. (You discussed this within your executive committee, remember?)

If you're honest with yourself, you'll have to acknowledge some of your sales hires do not present a success trajectory at all. They are better represented by that static point—that dot—you saw a little earlier.

If the success trajectory is not there, the most important question is not how to assign blame for what a given salesperson has done in the past but rather what you as the sales leader intend to do about the situation now. Fixating on past missteps at the expense of present strategy is known as "yelling at the scoreboard."

Let's leave aside for the moment the important question of whether you can expect to turn someone who currently has a dot or a down-and-to-the-right arrow into someone who has an up-and-to-the-right success trajectory. (The short answer here is that sometimes you can, but not always. We'll share details on that later.) Right now, our job is to give you the tools you need to conduct a critical reality check: How close does your current sales team come to the standard of your ideal sales hire?

Your ideal sales hire, by definition, is always motivated to move up and to the right—and you may well have hired people who don't match that criterion. The names you wrote down of the three people who weren't in the upper-right quadrant of the willing-and-able matrix are clear evidence of this.

Remember, we are talking about a trajectory. Because the members of your team are human, there will be times when they fall back. That goes for even the best people. There will be times when they run into obstacles, sometimes as the result of life challenges outside of the workplace and sometimes as the result of workplace changes that take some getting used to: new processes, new products, new skill requirements, and so on. Even top performers must work hard to maintain that up-and-to-the-right trajectory—and even top performers can fall back prior to moving forward again. But the motivation to get onto a success trajectory is what defines the people in the upper-right quadrant, even though they may experience temporary setbacks.

"The brave soul can mend even disaster."

–CATHERINE THE GREAT, RUSSIAN EMPRESS

These setbacks are no surprise to sales leaders. They are part of the terrain. The key questions are: Is this person sustaining the momentum needed to produce a success trajectory? And what, specifically, does the success trajectory for this position look like in practical terms?

That second question is the one we want to focus on closely right now.

What kind of person are you looking for? What traits does the ideal sales hire always possess, no matter what industry you're in or what your market looks like? Here's the 30,000-foot answer, which you should already be able to give: They possess willingness and ability. Here's how that answer breaks down.

Before You Hire Someone, Ask: "Is This Person Willing?"

Whether someone is really willing depends on that individual's behaviors and attitudes. Regardless of your industry, regardless of your product or service, the predictable behaviors and attitudes of the success trajectory hire will always include:

- **Desire.** This person is self-motivated and strongly goal-oriented. This person is a self-starter.
- **Drive.** This person persists in the face of adversity—and is often inspired by it. They do not rest on past achievements, but are goal-focused and always moving forward. Important: Someone who is not oriented toward moving up and to the right in terms of personal and professional development is not willing in the cultural sense.

- **Coachability.** You want someone who is open to coaching—not necessarily from you, although that's fine, but from someone. A person who is open to coaching is someone who is always looking to improve. This is a hallmark of a person who is trying to move up and to the right. Important: Someone who is not coachable, who believes they already have all the answers, is not on the success trajectory.

- **Possibility mindset.** This person operates from the assumption that there is plenty of success to go around, and that adversity is an opportunity to learn and improve, to push oneself and grow as a person. A possibility mindset is the opposite of a scarcity mindset, which is the mindset that dictates there is a limited number of achievements and resources. (Human beings determine their reality by means of their choice to occupy a possibility mindset or a scarcity mindset.)

- **Company focus.** This individual understands and is completely aligned with the organizational mission. They are thinking and acting on behalf of the company's best interests, and consistently act in accordance with the company culture, even when (especially when!) stressed or confused.

- **Team focus.** This person thinks we-first before thinking me-first. There is no sense of personal entitlement, no sense that "rules are for other people." Important: Someone who believes that rules are for other people is not willing in the cultural sense.

Management Courage Moment, Part One

Accept that if a candidate—or a current team member—is consistently missing even one of these elements to being willing, then they do not belong on your sales team. Even if the individual produces revenue, they are impeding your company's growth.

Before You Hire Someone, Ask: "Is This Person Able?"

Whether someone is able depends on that individual's techniques and applications. The predictable techniques and applications of the success trajectory hire will vary widely from team to team and industry to industry, but they will always include:

- **Creates and sustains relationships.** This person knows how to connect and interact effectively with a variety of behavioral styles.

- **Understands and executes a documentable sales process that includes forecasting accuracy.** This person has mastered the process by which leads turn into revenue for your sales team. Not only that: This person could write that process down in such a way that what showed up on their sheet of paper would match the process followed by other people who are producing consistently on your team. As a result of understanding and executing against a best practice sales process (for your company and product), this person does not over-commit or underperform in comparison with forecast.

- **Effective communication, both internal and external.** This individual communicates on an adult-to-adult level and does not take things personally. They know that the workplace is not the place to get one's emotional needs met. This person is collaborative and knows how to determine whether people are on the same page. This person follows up voice-to-voice contact with appropriate text and email communication and uses those tools effectively to reinforce key messages.

- **Negotiation, both internal and external.** This person does not shy away from difficult conversations. They know that conflict can sometimes be an effective tool for negotiating compromise, but never use conflict in a way that demeans others. (A side note: Too many salespeople, and even some sales leaders, waste time and energy negotiating internally against settled policy, rather than having a simple adult-to-adult conversation with the customer. Internal negotiating is fine in principle, and it does have its place, but it is often a cop-out for inexperienced salespeople and leaders. This is a down-and-to-the-left pattern.)

- **Effectively sets and defends Up-Front Contracts.** This is a critical cultural component, both within the sales team and in interactions with prospects and customers. Setting and defending an up-front contract simply means establishing and upholding a mutual agreement, also known as an agenda, so there can be an effective conversation with no mystery. The specifics of an up-front contract are pretty simple (see text box on the next page). Just remember that this individual sets the agenda for important discussions collaboratively, and then defends that agenda.

- **Analytics focus.** This person monitors and tracks personal and team activity by means of measurable daily, weekly, monthly, and quarterly outcomes. Focusing on things that can be counted gives everyone an accurate picture of what has

An Up-Front Contract includes five elements:

1. The purpose of the discussion.
2. The other person's agenda for the discussion, and their expectations of the salesperson before and during the discussion.
3. The salesperson's agenda for the meeting, and their expectations of the other person before and during the discussion.
4. The date, location, and duration of the discussion. Both parties should know when it will start and when it will end.
5. The expected outcome of the discussion.

taken place. The numbers should give clear insights on what has happened up to this point, what has worked, what hasn't, and what action you need to take to create no-drama action plans for what needs to happen next. When focusing on the numbers is part of your culture, it's much easier to have discussions about concrete actions, rather than about who is right and who is wrong, who is up or who is down, who is good or who is bad. The numbers are what they are.

- **Customer and business acumen.** This person knows how to identify and articulate personal and business pain and also how to build effective alliances with people in the organization who support the delivery of measurable value to the customer. This person works collaboratively with those people to create powerful business relationships.

"Sure, most salespeople have decent rapport and selling skills. That's just the beginning. The truly excellent ones raise their game by working as a team with other functions within their organization to build and prove extraordinary value to their buyers. These salespeople consistently produce in the top tier. They have both business acumen and customer acumen, which means simply that they know how to form good working alliances with people in marketing, product development, customer success, and other functions to illustrate the customer journey and articulate what life looks like after the contract is signed. This trait is critical to high-level success. Too many so-called 'lone wolves' completely ignore this aspect of their job, leaving money on the table."

–JILL ROWLEY, PARTNER AT STAGE 2 CAPITAL; FORMER CHIEF GROWTH OFFICER

Management Courage Moment, Part Two

Accept that if a candidate—or a current team member—is consistently missing even one of these elements of being able, then they do not belong on your sales team.

Key Takeaways

- A candidate or current team member who presents the trajectory of being willing to do the job of selling has desire, has drive, is coachable, has a possibility mindset, and maintains both a company focus and a team focus.

- A candidate or current team member who presents the trajectory of being able to do the job of selling creates and sustains bonding and rapport, understands and executes a documentable sales process, communicates effectively (both internally and externally), negotiates effectively (both internally and externally), effectively sets and defends up-front contracts, and has a strong analytics focus.

Your Commitment

- Accept that if a candidate—or a current team member—is consistently missing even one of these elements to being willing or able—for instance, because of a pattern of blaming others or a pattern of failing to follow through on agreed-upon action steps—then they do not belong on your sales team. (Note: This is a management courage moment.)

CHAPTER FOURTEEN

Your Ideal
Sales Hire, Continued

THE VISUAL EXPRESSION OF EVERYTHING you learned in the prior chapters about your ideal sales hire looks like the willing-and-able matrix on the next page.

It is vitally important that this simple, powerful visual model becomes your weekly and quarterly touchpoint with each member of the sales team. Everyone on the team should know where they stand in relation to this model and in what direction they are headed at all times. Because the success or failure of your internal revolution depends largely on the internal prominence of this information graphic, we're going to be reminding you of it regularly.

The Success Cadence℠ WILLING-AND-ABLE MATRIX

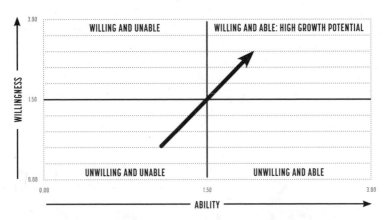

Is This Person Willing?
(Behavior & Attitude)

- Desire
- Drive
- Coachability
- Possibility mindset
  (as opposed to scarcity mindset)
- Company focus
- Team focus
- No entitlement mindset

Is This Person Able?
(Technique & Application)

Skills will vary by specific position, but basic skills always include:

- Strong communication, both internal and external
- Executes a documentable sales process
- Negotiation skills, both internal and external
- Sets and defends Up-Front Contract, bonding and rapport
- Analytics (monitor and track personal activity with measurable daily, weekly, quarterly outcomes)
- Customer and business acumen

"Designing an information graphic, a visual display of data or phenomena, is a moral act. We should strive for clarity, rigor, and depth. That's the way to regain the credibility we've lost as a community."

−ALBERTO CAIRO, SPANISH INFORMATION DESIGNER AND PROFESSOR

Your job now is a simple one. Continue the process you started in Chapter 11. Using the criteria we've just shared with you, award each current member of your sales team a score of 0 to 3 for each of the "willing" and "able" factors that will help you to identify your ideal sales hire. A score of 0 means you have seen no evidence of the attribute. A score of 3 means this trait is already a predictable and consistent part of this person's approach to the job for which they have been hired.

Here's an example of a scorecard you can use for each salesperson. It follows a very simple system. Yours may be different, of course. The most effective sales leaders construct these collaboratively with their teams.

0: Too new to rate **1:** Cannot perform this **2:** Can perform this **3:** Can teach this to others				
Willingness				
Desire: Self-starter	0	1	2	3
Drive: Sees adversity as a challenge	0	1	2	3
Coachable	0	1	2	3
Possibility mindset (not scarcity mindset)	0	1	2	3
Company focus (aligned with company mission)	0	1	2	3
Team focus (no entitlement)	0	1	2	3
Ability (Note: Techniques and applications will vary by specific position, but basic skills will always include the below.)				
Communication (internal and external)	0	1	2	3
Executes a documentable sales process	0	1	2	3
Negotiation (internal and external)	0	1	2	3
Establishes bonding and rapport	0	1	2	3
Sets and defends Up-Front Contracts	0	1	2	3
Analytics focus (monitors and tracks personal activity with measurable daily, weekly, quarterly outcomes)	0	1	2	3
Customer and business acumen (builds effective internal alliances, works collaboratively to create powerful business relationships)	0	1	2	3

Once you have done that assessment for each salesperson who reports to you, use the results you've generated to sort the current profiles of all the members of your present sales team into one of the four groups. (Assume that someone who scores 1 or lower for one of the "willing" elements is not yet willing. Assume someone who scores 1 or lower for one of the "able" elements is not yet able.)

- Unwilling and unable
- Willing and unable
- Unwilling and able
- Willing and able

This assessment, of course, is a snapshot of where each team member is right now; the more snapshots you collect over time, the clearer the trajectory is likely to be. This assessment is also confidential. Be sure to date it. Share it securely with the person you just had your executive committee meeting with—and ask for feedback.

Always make a point of measuring both willingness and ability monthly or quarterly so you can chart the person's long-term path and make sure that the person's direction (not the snapshot) is consistent with the success trajectory you want. These quantifiable monthly or quarterly measurements of activity and performance are vitally important, because they allow you to ensure that the salesperson—and the team as a whole—never loses momentum and never loses linearity. Linearity is consistent, predictable, steady revenue performance. It's the opposite of what happens when the team coasts for nine weeks, then turns on the engine and starts, in Weeks 10–12, trying to catch up on all the activity they should have been doing in Weeks 1–9.*

---

* An equally serious problem is the team member who makes the conscious choice to slow down or withhold reporting on a soon-to-close deal in order to make the next performance period look better. This is contrary to the working culture of rapid growth that drives the Success Cadence, and it should be identified, early on, as a fire-able offense.

Warning: Taking your snapshots annually, pretending they constitute a performance review, and then filing them away for 12 months is worse than useless. It's demotivating, and will drive good people away from your organization. Keep the lines of communication open!

Key Takeaway

- Monthly or quarterly assessments allow you to ensure that the salesperson—and the team as a whole—never loses momentum and never loses linearity: consistent, predictable revenue performance.

Your Commitment

- Measure both the willingness and ability of each team member using the tools in this chapter. Based on your assessment, create a snapshot of each person on your current sales staff as occupying one of the four quadrants: "willing and able," "willing and unable," "unwilling and able," "unwilling and unable." (Keep the assessments and any discussions about them confidential.)

CHAPTER FIFTEEN

The Art of Saying Goodbye

WHAT DO YOU DO WITH the information gained from the exercise in the prior chapter?

You start by putting it into context. Many truly great sales hires come in with very high willingness, but without any of the company-specific abilities. For instance, they may not yet know everything they need to know about the technical specifications of whatever it is you sell or about how it's serviced. That's natural. You have to take all of that into account as you evaluate potential sales hires.

But if you don't see clear, unmistakable evidence of an up-and-to-the-right trajectory in the past jobs this person has held or if the person shows a poor or dubious fit with any of the other elements of the template you've laid out for this position, then you have to accept that maybe there's not a good match here. You have to say goodbye to the applicant, even if you have a good gut feeling about the person. This is one of the issues you have an obligation to be tactful but clear about when you set expectations with a job applicant at the beginning of an interview.

When it comes to evaluating new hires, understand that lots of people are likely to come in at the upper-left quadrant—"willing and unable." The question is, will that person stay there? If you hire the right person, a truly coachable person, the answer is always going to be "no way." If their willingness stays high and their ability ramps, that person will move horizontally to the right, to "willing and able." By the way, after you learn this system and make it second nature, you as a leader will be able to predict how long it will take for that to happen. Whenever the company innovates, whenever markets change, whenever brand new markets are opened up, it's natural for salespeople to fall back to high willingness and low ability—until they are trained.

The question isn't whether there's going to be movement between those two boxes. There is. The question is whether you can hire someone who won't be satisfied until they move back into the upper-right quadrant. If you don't have clear proof that you're looking at such a person, don't make a job offer.

There is a lot still to come about the process that you need to establish to make a rapid-growth hiring and retention culture a scalable reality for your sales team. There is, however, a critical point to understand in order to make that process work: Your job as sales leader is to disqualify, not to qualify.

Yes, you're constantly looking for new prospective hires—but at the same time, you're constantly looking for reasons to say "no." You're looking for reasons to say "goodbye, thank you, good luck." You're looking for proof that the person you're considering doesn't fit your template. That's very different from assuming that the person you're interviewing does fit the template, which is what happens in a slow-growth culture.

The quicker you get to *no*, the quicker you can locate someone who's a *yes*. That's the guiding recruitment idea in a rapid-growth culture. By the way, it's also the guiding sales idea in a rapid-growth culture. This is exactly the dynamic you want your salespeople to follow with prospects. You want them to go for the *no*. You want them to have a clear template of what the ideal prospect looks like, and you want them to follow a process that helps them clearly identify the people who don't qualify as ideal buyers—so they can spend their time with the people who do.

So, now that you know that horizontal movement between the top two boxes is not only normal, but healthy—now that you know the big issue is whether the person stays in the top half of the matrix—you know that someone who routinely spends most of the time in the bottom half of the matrix is not going to get you where you, your team, or your company want to go. That's not who you want to hire.

The bottom half of the matrix is the zone where willingness slows to a trickle (or vanishes altogether) and coachability is nonexistent.

The bottom half of the matrix shows you the people below the willingness line—the people to whom you must say goodbye.

Herb Brooks would not recruit these people and would not hang onto them. Neither should you.

Too many salespeople spend most of their time below the willingness line. They may keep themselves very busy, but week after week, month after month, their actions, attitudes, and results somehow don't match up with what you expected when you hired them. By their continuous presence below the willingness line, they are letting you know, in no uncertain terms, that they are not a good match for your team or your company. It is your job to act on that message.

> *"Don't mistake activity for achievement."*
> **–JOHN WOODEN, AMERICAN ATHLETE, COACH, AND AUTHOR**

There is an art to saying goodbye gracefully to applicants (and employees) who don't match your template. We can't tell you what graceful words to say in any given situation. We can only tell you that you do need to learn to say the words. If you master the art of saying goodbye, you are leading a rapid-growth culture. If you don't, you aren't. Understand this much, and you are ready to implement everything that follows.

It's not realistic to expect continuous upper-right-quadrant performance, week in and week out. It is realistic to expect a continuous, predictable trajectory towards the upper-right quadrant of the willing-and-able matrix.

Now that you know that, you have the foundation of an effective recruitment, hiring, and retention program. We'll talk about the nuts and bolts of such a program a little bit later in the book. Right now, you are ready to look in depth at a critical question about your current staff, one that we raised a little earlier: Can you expect to turn around someone who clearly doesn't have an up-and-to-the-right trajectory?

We'll address that issue in the next chapter.

Key Takeaways

- The best salespeople, the people you want to hire and hold onto, fluctuate horizontally in the top two boxes, above the willingness line. The people you don't want to hire and hold onto spend most of their time below that line.
- Abilities fluctuate depending on speed of change, and willingness can fluctuate based on what is going on in the person's life. The basic trajectory of a good sales hire, however, should be up and to the right.
- Your job as sales leader is to disqualify, not to qualify.
- You must learn to say goodbye to people currently on staff who prove that their pattern is to spend most or all of their time below the willingness line.

Your Commitment

- Identify someone specific on your team who is on the success trajectory but whose willingness or ability once temporarily shifted out of the upper-right quadrant of the willing-and-able matrix for some reason. Recall why that happened and how the person got back on track.
- Create a confidential, preliminary list of the salespeople on your present team that you should say goodbye to. Share this list with your accountability partner. Get feedback.

CHAPTER SIXTEEN

Turning Around Someone without a Success Trajectory

CAN YOU TURN AROUND SOMEONE on your sales team who clearly doesn't have a success trajectory? The simple, cut-to-the-chase answer to this question is: Probably not. And that's on you. (A side note: shame on you as a sales leader if you do not change the status quo in order to make sure your people have the proper tools for success: an effective onboarding and enablement program that gets the new hire to full potential; continuous measurement against well understood, best practice milestones; a continuous education mentality, with money behind it; and regular coaching. Otherwise, your next hire will fail, too.)

It's not impossible to turn around a failure trajectory. But the important question really isn't whether this is possible. The question is whether you should invest the time and effort required. To figure that out, you need to have a clear sense of which person and which performance quadrant you're talking about.

Unwilling and Unable

Let's be frank here. The question that appears at the top of this chapter typically doesn't arise because a manager wants to hold onto people in this quadrant. People who have shown clearly over time that they belong in the unwilling-and-unable category represent a pretty easy decision. If you know for certain that an individual in this category isn't able do the job and isn't willing to try, it's time for both of you to move on. (That includes someone who floats from "willing and unable" to "unwilling and unable.") The plan in such cases is simple: immediate removal.

What about the other quadrants? Let's look at each of them next.

Willing and Unable

What should you, as the sales leader, do about someone on your team who has established a clear pattern of showing up in the willing-and-unable quadrant? (By the way, this is the only gray area, in our view. The questions about what to do in all of the other quadrants pretty much answer themselves.)

Here are some action items to consider in the case of the willing-and-unable performer. As you review them, bear in mind that someone who is new to the role and still orienting themselves to the responsibilities of the job may simply need your support, guidance, and patience to launch an up-and-to-the-right trajectory.

- Confirm that you have set the right baselines for the person's daily, weekly, and monthly behavioral targets. (We'll talk in much more detail about this in Chapter 24.)

- Train this person. Make sure this person gets the training and ongoing reinforcement they need to master the relevant skills. You don't have to do the training yourself, but you do have to make sure it happens. Identify the three or four most important skills necessary for success in this role, and make sure there is competency in each.

- Coach this person effectively, so that you uncover hidden obstacles that may be preventing the up-and-to-the-right trajectory from presenting itself.

- Supervise this person. Keep close track of the numbers and activities. Is the performance trend changing or staying the same? Based on what you can document, create appropriate behavioral plans, collaborate on goal setting, and set clear expectations. You could also pair this person with a high contributor.

- Reward this person in such a way as to help them fulfill important personal goals. This presupposes that you know what those goals are, of course. (That's part of the coaching conversation.)

- Reassign* this person or part company if there is no change in the trajectory after an extended period of time. (Only you can define what an "extended period of time" is in your team or your organization. For us, two consecutive quarters without any change in the trajectory would be a major problem, and a signal that it is time to say goodbye.

Unwilling and Able

Now for the big issue—the one that is likely to test your courage as a manager. When sales leaders ask if a salesperson who doesn't have a success trajectory can be turned around, it's usually because they are eager to find a way to hold onto a high performer with entitlement issues who falls into the unwilling-and-able quadrant.

Many people we talk to have already rationalized a decision to keep such a person on staff, on the theory that this salesperson's willingness will somehow improve. These managers may hope to be able to keep experiencing positive outcomes, such as the closing of major deals, without developing the deep talent pool that will keep them from over-relying on a single team member. They may simply not be comfortable saying goodbye to people. Or, they may have both of these issues to deal with. All these leaders really end up doing, however, is creating a negative sales culture that keeps scalable growth from happening.

Before you look past the cultural problem; before you start

---

* It's entirely possible this individual may thrive in another role, and you are within your rights to reach that conclusion. However, if you do opt to reassign the person, be sure to make a full disclosure to the team getting them. Otherwise, you are passing the buck, a habit best reserved for your competitors.

making excuses for a salesperson who is clearly able to close business but is just as clearly unwilling to adopt the we-first outlook essential to a scalable sales process; before you move into denial—you have to do the following things.

- **Be brutally honest about entitlement issues.** A sense of entitlement means that the individual expects to be able to play by different rules than the rest of the team. Someone with an entitlement mindset is by definition unwilling to do the job your team culture demands. Such a person is a potential blight on the team and the organization, and how you deal with them is a critical test for you as a sales leader. (We will examine in depth how to handle this test in the next chapter, "Your Cultural Moment of Truth.")

- **Look past the short-term wins.** Think in the long term. Think about scalability. A series of short-term revenue infusions from this person is not worth sabotaging the team's willing-and-able culture, which is the bedrock of the Success Cadence revolution you are leading.

- **Know when to part company.** One quarter with someone on the team whom you know for certain has entitlement issues is one quarter too long. In all cases in which someone needs to be removed from a role, it's imperative that you as the sales leader take care of the problem before someone else forces you to. You are the person best positioned to know when there is a problem, and you are the likeliest source of effective action that results in the least disruption to revenue, morale, and budget. A CEO, functional head, or even a board member may apply pressure if they conclude that you're not handling a problem expeditiously. Don't wait for that to happen. Do it yourself, proactively. Lead. That way you'll never have to worry about upsetting your cadence or that of your team.

"Being fired has some of the advantages of dying without its supreme disadvantages. People say extra-nice things about you, and you get to hear them."

–HOWARD ZINN, AMERICAN HISTORIAN

Key Takeaway

- Say goodbye to people who prove that they consistently show up in the unwilling-and-unable category.
- Consider working with people in the willing-and-unable category for up to two quarters. If they don't turn around, say goodbye.
- Say goodbye to people with entitlement issues who prove that they consistently show up in the unwilling-and-able category.

Your Commitment

- Identify someone specific on your team who has exhibited entitlement issues. Discuss this person with your accountability partner.

CHAPTER SEVENTEEN

Your Cultural Moment of Truth

WE'VE BEEN TALKING A LOT about management moments of courage. These are moments when you are called on to do something you know is right, even though it takes you out of your personal comfort zone. It's basically something you know you need to do but are deeply uncomfortable doing. It's time to share a salesperson-specific management moment of courage now: the moment when you say goodbye to someone you know isn't a good fit for your culture, your team, or your organization—someone with entitlement issues who is also bringing significant revenue into the organization.

For too many sales leaders, this is a blind spot—a problem they don't acknowledge because at some level they don't want to acknowledge it. Or, perhaps it is a problem that they acknowledge but convince themselves isn't yet a major priority. In either case, the result is the same—they rationalize the issue into insignificance, fail to connect with the reality of the situation, and do nothing. They allow two different sets of performance standards to prevail: one for the person with entitlement issues, and another for everyone else. The financial contribution causes them to look the other way when it's time to defend a single standard; very often they're focused on issues that seem more pressing, and they tell themselves they'll deal with the problem later. Does this ring any bells?

There are major negative consequences to indulging the entitlement blind spot in this way. Others around you may assume that you have simply chosen to ignore the problem indefinitely, which leads to a deepening morale problem on the team. As the infractions get worse, you find you eventually do have to come to grips with the situation—but by the time you realize that, you have multiple fences to mend and major cultural problems to address. Maybe you decide to put off dealing with it for another month to see what happens. That's called a downward cycle. It kills team performance.

This common downward cycle is rooted in one thing: inconsistency. Inconsistency is a common factor in a slow-growth sales culture. When you treat people on your sales team inconsistently, you may tell yourself that this inconsistency is a minor issue—but it isn't. Inconsistencies in performance standards, even seemingly minor ones, are what cause people to lose respect for the company and for you as the leader. You simply can't afford it.

The moment you recognize the real-world consequences of

inconsistency is always difficult. But the moment you take clear steps to rectify that inconsistency in both the short term and the long term is always a major turning point. This moment represents a critical change of direction for those leaders who are truly committed to creating and supporting a rapid-growth working culture for the sales team—and, indeed, for the entire organization. By not changing direction at this critical moment, you ensure that a rapid-growth sales culture is impossible to sustain in your organization.

At the end of this chapter, we're going to ask you to make this cultural moment of truth happen on your team by first planning it out and discussing it with your executive committee and then taking action with a member of your sales team. Do not wing it when it comes to this moment of truth. Read the example we share in this chapter. It will help you make your moment of truth a reality. Once you've done that, take this cultural moment of truth and plan it out in detail for your own team with the help of your executive committee. Then, execute it without hesitation or second thoughts.

This is often easier said than done. Who wants to lose a top performer? When you start thinking about what your cultural moment of truth entails, it may not feel natural to your leadership style. Imagining actually doing it, now, may take you out of your comfort zone as a manager and a leader. The prospect of taking direct action on the commitment you will find at the end of this chapter may initially feel like something you should postpone for a while, until you have a little more experience and a little more information.

Our challenge to you is to recognize these responses for what they are: reminders that your past does not have to equal your future.

You have moved out of your comfort zone before. You can move out of your comfort zone now. In fact, you must. Any rationalization you find yourself making is a sign that you have a choice to stay within your comfort zone or move outside of it. Once you recognize that, you will recognize you should do this sooner, rather than later. Make planning for this cultural moment of truth the subject of your second voice-to-voice meeting with your accountability partner just as soon as possible.

This is your cultural moment of truth. If you haven't had it yet (and most of the leaders we work with haven't), it's a solid bet that your sales team is not growing as fast as it could be.

In our experience, something like the decision you'll be reading about next has to happen in order to sustain a working culture that:

- Supports individual team members in achieving their full potential.
- Increases the possibility for aggressive revenue growth for the team as a whole.
- Makes that growth scalable over time.

Kevin and Paul, or the Template for Your Cultural Moment of Truth

The scenario you are about to read is a combination of events and decisions we have seen play out at dozens of selling organizations that have successfully made the transition into a rapid-growth working culture. This narrative lays out what the cultural moment of truth looked like for a fictional sales manager, Kevin, who had not yet implemented the principles of this book.

Kevin led a team of 20 salespeople at Freedonia Group. His team included Paul, a top performer who was also a living, breathing, walking personification of drama waiting for a reason to happen.

Paul had been with the company for nine months. Kevin just couldn't seem to create a good one-on-one discussion with him—which was odd, given that the two had hit it off great during Paul's job interview. For three years now, ever since he'd been recruited as sales manager, Kevin had prided himself on his ability to connect with people, identify what was really going on, support his team, and maintain a positive working environment for everyone. But lately, that had become more and more difficult to do. Kevin had a growing sense that Paul was part of the reason for that. Now, nearly a year in, it was becoming clearer and clearer that Paul was a disruptive force on Kevin's team.

It hadn't started out that way. After a brilliant phone interview followed by an equally brilliant in-person interview, Paul had stood out from the pack—and Kevin had had a very good feeling about him. His gut told him this was a major contributor. He hired Paul right away, on the strength of the exemplary track record detailed on his resume and Paul's ample list of contacts within a key target industry where he'd once worked as a salesperson. Paul hit the ground running, posting the best revenue figures for his first 60 days of anyone in the company's history. He quickly emerged as the top producer in the department, selling a large percentage of his deals to personal contacts from the previous position at the other company. His average deal size was well above that of all the other team members, which was remarkable for a new hire.

The trouble was, the better Paul did in terms of bringing in revenue, the more he seemed to regard himself as the final authority on policy and procedure.

This problem had started out small—he started missing the deadline for filing a weekly activity report. Kevin would send out a gentle reminder via email, and the report would eventually show up—but the next week, the pattern would repeat itself with an even longer delay. At first, Kevin told himself that discretion was the better part of valor in such a situation, that it made sense to cut someone with Paul's potential a little slack. But now Kevin realized that he hadn't seen an activity report from Paul for several months. Not only that: Kevin was able to confirm that Paul was completely ignoring the tools, resources, and activity targets that had been set up for identifying new contacts, opportunities, and, ultimately, customers. After exhausting his personal contact list, Paul had simply done no new to keep his revenue stream going.

There were other issues, and they were becoming increasingly difficult to ignore. Paul routinely missed meetings. He didn't even pretend to update the CRM, which was a must for all team members. He didn't attend biweekly interdepartmental meetings with the marketing team. He improvised his way through the team's carefully designed and documented sales process—following the playbook when he felt comfortable doing so and ignoring the playbook when he didn't. He was unresponsive and uncooperative during one-on-one debriefs. All of these instances connected to basic parts of the job, things that everyone else on the team had to do.

When Kevin tried talking privately to Paul about these issues, there was always some kind of drama to deal with, some new complaint to evaluate, some perceived slight or misdeed from one of the other team members that had caused Paul to act as he had. Up to this point Kevin had put up with all the awkwardness because Paul was producing at a very high level. In just nine months, in fact, he had landed three of the biggest deals in the company's history. Yes, Paul was arrogant. Yes, he clearly considered himself the lead dog on the sled team. But wasn't making the quarterly target what it was all about? And hadn't Paul been the one who had made the difference in hitting team quota last quarter? Didn't the top person on the team get to be treated like the alpha dog once in a while?

So Kevin had let things slide. He had worked on the assumption that a team with someone like Paul, someone who was now routinely posting revenue totals that were 20% above the numbers of anyone else on the team, was better than a team without someone like Paul.

Then came the crisis.

One Monday morning, Kevin showed up for work and got an email marked "confidential." Its attachment was a PDF signed by both Salvador, Kevin's most experienced veteran performer who had been with the company for nearly 10 years, and Mazie, his tech expert who had once worked in product development and made a successful transition into the world of sales a little over two years before. The PDF announced that they were each resigning, effective 30 days from then.

Why? The resignation letter explained that Salvador and Mazie felt they couldn't continue working in an office where there were two different sets of performance standards in place: the written standards (outlined in the department's orientation process, its employee handbook, and its operating manual) and the unwritten standard that Paul got to play by.

Kevin took a deep breath. He knew deep down that they were absolutely right. He had allowed two different sets of standards to emerge. He had shifted his approach to leading the team after Paul came on board. He had told himself that there were good reasons for doing that, including the difficult challenge of keeping up with a changing and unpredictable market environment. So, yes, he had allowed Paul to play by a different set of rules on the little things. He assumed this wasn't a particularly big deal. Now he wasn't so sure. If Salvador and Mazie had decided to form a united front on this issue, it was certain that others on the team were feeling the same kind of resentment. Did that mean he was going to start losing good people in droves now? Paul was good—but he wasn't good enough to make up for a deficit like that.

Kevin suddenly realized that he was in trouble. There was no way to keep the sales team on track, much less hit the aggressive "hockey stick" growth goal he had promised CEO Diane that he could deliver, with this kind of uprising in the works. Although Kevin suspected that the 30-day timeline he had been offered was a signal that these two key performers really did want to find a way to stay on, he felt he had no time to waste. He closed his door and called Diane's extension.

Diane's assistant, Preston, picked up. Kevin asked for a one-on-one meeting with her over lunch at an off-site location, as soon as possible. When Preston suggested "sometime next week," Kevin politely requested something sooner. This was an emergency, he explained. There was a major problem on the sales team, and he needed Diane's help in assessing it and resolving it. Was there any chance he could manage a meeting with her today?

Preston put him on hold for a moment. When he came back on line, he told Kevin that the only available slot Diane had was over lunch. Would that work? It sure would!

That day, as Diane and Kevin met at a nearby diner to discuss the email Kevin had received, Diane agreed that this was in fact an emergency. She told Kevin that she was glad that he'd gotten in touch about it immediately. Diane asked him what he'd learned from what had happened.

Kevin was up front about where he'd made mistakes. He had looked the other way and rationalized his decision to "cut Paul some slack" on things like filing activity reports because Paul was bringing in good revenue. He realized now that this rationalization had somehow morphed into a decision to allow Paul to write his own playbook, and as a result he was now facing a serious morale issue within the department, paired with a potentially devastating turnover challenge. This problem had been building up for months. Kevin had simply failed to notice it.

Diane thanked Kevin for his honesty, then admitted that she wasn't sure what to do either. After some discussion, the two came to the difficult conclusion that, although letting Paul go would mean that the revenue picture for the coming quarter was certainly going to look worse, it was the only way to support the longer-term income picture and the company goals that Diane and Kevin had taken on for

Freedonia. Kevin discussed with Diane all the times he had already tried to bring Paul up to speed, and they agreed he'd been given fair warning. They could keep Paul on, have a decent quarter, and a deeply dysfunctional team—or let him go, have a difficult quarter now, and have a more functional team with the potential for higher performance in the months and years to come. They opted for the latter.

Diane suggested, and Kevin agreed, that the first step was for Kevin to reach out to Salvador and Mazie to thank them for putting these issues on his radar screen, to ask them to put their decision on hold for 48 hours, and to not discuss their email with others while Kevin worked out the next steps with regard to Paul's status at the company. Diane would then get the paperwork moving and initiate the correct procedures, and Kevin would begin the process of parting company with Paul. Once Paul was gone, Kevin would communicate to the staff his recommitment to the importance of there being a single set of standards for everyone. He would ask for their help in holding himself accountable to deliver on that standard as a manager.

After nearly 90 minutes at the diner, both Kevin and Diane felt good about this path. "This decision isn't just because of the longer-term financial impact of keeping someone like Paul," Diane pointed out, "and it isn't just because we want to hold onto two good team members. Paul needs to go for a much bigger reason: You and I have an obligation to defend the positive working culture of this organization. If we held onto Paul, he would be an obstacle to us becoming the kind of company we want to be. And, he would make it more likely that other members of the sales team would become obstacles. Taking a short-term financial hit to make sure that doesn't happen is worth it to me."

Within 48 hours of receiving that email from Salvador and Mazie, Kevin got the OK from Diane. He called Paul into his office and said goodbye, with no drama since Kevin knew how to handle it professionally and unemotionally. Upon hearing this news, Salvador and Mazie rescinded their resignations.

The next morning, another team member, Ito—a bright and enthusiastic new hire who had come on only 60 days before and was off to a great start—told Kevin privately that he was glad to see Paul go. When Kevin asked why that was, Ito said, "Because I was afraid that Paul was the kind of guy I would have to become in order to do well at this company—and I really didn't want to become that kind of guy."

"Run to the fire; don't hide from it."

—MEG WHITMAN, CEO AND PRESIDENT, HEWLETT PACKARD

Kevin Was Lucky

This fictional example is based on countless real-life cases of perceived entitlement we have encountered over the years. We realize, as we hope you do, that the crisis that landed on Kevin's lap—in the form of an email from two valued members of the team—was actually a major stroke of luck for him. That email shone a spotlight on the true cost of letting a salesperson who is producing but is degrading the working culture of the team as a whole remain on the payroll.

You can't assume you will be that lucky.

You can't assume you'll get an email.

You must reach out to senior leadership within your organization before there's a crisis. You must take steps now to identify and execute a plan for either terminating or sending a clear "shape up or ship out" message to any salesperson on your team who reflects Paul's entitled me-first attitude. You must make sure senior leadership is on your side. Finally, you must stand by your actions. Doing this will send all the right messages to the people on your sales team. Failing to do so will send all the wrong messages.

A scalable, rapid-growth culture on your sales team is impossible until you have parted company with any salesperson who consistently brings their entitlement issues to the workplace. Typically, parting company with one such salesperson is enough to send the right message and defend the right working culture.

Here is a reality check. In our experience, it takes someone actually being disciplined or losing a position for the rest of the team to understand that having an attitude of entitlement has no place in your working culture, on your sales team, or in your organization. Parting company works best. Your moment of truth—and the biggest management courage moment thus far—is to meet now with your executive committee, set up the plan, and then part company with any salesperson on your team who exhibits these tendencies. If you have already done this and your team has already processed the implications of that leadership decision, congratulations. You are now in a position to defend an up-and-to-the-right working culture. If you haven't done this, it's time to get to work and take action on this management courage moment.

"A moment of choice is a moment of truth. It's the testing point of our character and competence."

–STEPHEN COVEY, AMERICAN EDUCATOR, AUTHOR, BUSINESSMAN, AND SPEAKER

Key Takeaway

- A scalable, rapid-growth culture on your sales team is impossible until you have parted company with any salesperson who brings an attitude of entitlement to the workplace. Typically, parting company with one such salesperson is enough to send the right message and defend the right working culture.

Your Commitment

- Make planning for this cultural moment of truth the subject of your second voice-to-voice meeting with your accountability partner. Then, execute the plan without second guessing yourself. Say "goodbye" to a salesperson with entitlement issues.

CHAPTER EIGHTEEN

Why You Say Goodbye

THE FICTIONAL EXAMPLE WE SHARED with you in the previous chapter—a sales leader working with top leadership to decide it is time to part company with a top performer not taking the actions necessary to support the team's success—is more than just an interesting story. It represents a real-life turning point for every sales organization that ends up embracing and capitalizing on a rapid-growth sales culture. Again: If you haven't gone through something like this, you need to. There are three main reasons this is so.

First and foremost, this experience sends and supports the critical message that everyone must play by the same set of rules. Meaning, you act as a team and you all follow the same playbook. A rapid-growth culture that supports the entire sales team is impossible to sustain if the team doesn't believe everyone is playing by the same set of rules. They must not only believe but consistently act on the assumption that this is the case. Letting someone go who doesn't adopt this team mindset sends an unmistakable signal to everyone that you are serious. If someone doesn't follow the playbook everyone else has to follow, if they keep trying to make up their own rules as they go along, their job is in jeopardy. Once you as the sales leader defend the policy that everyone plays by the same set of rules, behavior changes.

"You can work anywhere, but over time I have found it is is a lot more fun working for a company that is growing instead of shrinking"
– ALEX SHOOTMAN, CEO, WORKFRONT

Once the principle that you are willing to fire someone over this is accepted as a central operating principle of the team, the whole workplace dynamic—the whole approach to work—changes. One way or another, a we-first mindset emerges. You'll be able to count on each of the members of your sales team to do one of two things: 1) they will also defend that we-first working culture, in ways large and small, because they prefer working and succeeding in a we-first environment, or 2) they will quietly start looking for another place to work because they know they're not a good match culturally, and they'd rather leave than get fired. Either is a great outcome.

Second, this experience sends the right message to the members of the sales team about what their job really is. Once there has been a termination that clarifies that people can in fact lose their job for not being a team player, salespeople start to take the whole concept of team performance a lot more seriously. They begin to realize that hitting team goals and supporting team initiatives really is a critical part of their job description. As a result, they begin doing a better job of supporting each other.

> *"We are talking, ultimately, about a cross-functional team focus. What are we going to do on a weekly/monthly/quarterly basis to make sure that we are keeping each other honest and accountable on making and executing the scaling decisions as a team? Are we making the decisions that will keep us on track with our individual plans, all the way through to the company strategic plans?"*
>
> **–JAMES MURRAY, SALES LEADER**

The compensation plan you choose has a major impact on this, of course. The salesperson's attitude toward their job and the other members of the team is always going to be connected to the formal compensation policies you implement, but it will also be connected to the priorities you set and defend. Firing Paul affects the team's attitude toward the job. After someone like Paul is let go, the remaining members of your team will realize that working together is not just something printed on a poster in the break room, but rather something they need to do on a consistent basis in order to fulfill their core job requirements. They realize their job isn't just to bring in revenue but rather to be part of a team that functions effectively in bringing in revenue. Grasping this distinction is an essential step toward creating a self-governing sales team, which is something we'll be looking at a lot more closely in Part 2 of this book.

Third, this experience sends the right message to you about what your job really is. This is vitally important. Before you actually go through an experience like the one Kevin and Diane had to go through in deciding to let go of Paul, you could be tempted to believe that the real issue in such a situation is the salesperson's sense of entitlement. But is it? Right now is a good time for you to stop and reconsider the essentials of your job.

You are a sales leader. Your job is to deliver a certain product, one that delivers revenue: salespeople who are both willing and able to do their job. Accepting this means being willing and able to ask yourself certain difficult but important questions. If you're Kevin and you've just gone through the difficult experience of letting Paul go, it makes sense to ask yourself:

- How did Paul get hired in the first place? Answer: Kevin hired him—and recall that he did so on the strength of his gut instinct, which in this case turned out to be wrong. Kevin alone interviewed Paul. Kevin alone made the decision to hire him, and he wasn't even screening for the we-first vs. me-first mindset. That means Kevin alone is personally responsible for the heavy costs associated with a bad sales hire, which the best sources now estimate, once you figure in the direct and indirect costs (such as opportunity costs), at between 10 and 20 times Paul's annual salary. Ouch!

  Reality check: The major issue here is not one salesperson's sense of entitlement, it's the recruiting and hiring process. Gut instinct hiring does not work. Hiring with only one person doing the interviewing does not work. Given the stakes, your standard must be to hire well and fire better. You'll learn a lot more about this standard in Part 2 of this book.

- What if everyone had been performing at or near Paul's level? If Kevin had had a staff full of people who were truly willing and able and who were highly motivated to achieve, would losing one contributor have made a huge difference to the team's income picture? Would it still have been a crisis? Answer: No. If you as a sales leader are doing your job at the optimum level—meaning the job of attracting and retaining only highly motivated people who are both willing and able—your staff would be delivering results at a level that keep you from being held hostage by a single top performer. Again—ouch!

  Reality check: The major issue here is not one salesperson's sense of entitlement—it's your recruiting and hiring process, coupled with your management process. You need scheduled talent assessments to confirm that everyone on your staff is moving up and to the right and to identify the very highest level performers. This is something you'll learn more about in Part 2.

- If Kevin had immediate access to an active network of candidates who could perform at Paul's level and who were personally eager to take Paul's place within 10 working days, would Paul's departure have been a crisis? Answer: No. The reason this was a crisis is that Kevin currently only focused on hiring when there was a vacancy or when there was an approved headcount in the budget. That's why Kevin went into "red alert" mode. This is a common leadership blind spot. As a sales leader, you do your best to put out the fire and then blissfully ignore the task of recruiting—until someone leaves, at which point the cycle repeats itself. As a result, you don't have an active network of people who are eager to get onto your sales team. It's your responsibility to have that kind of network because, remember, salespeople who are willing and able are the product you supply. If you are not looking at your team members' willing-and-able matrixes on a quarterly basis and planning to take action when anyone's trajectory shows a lack of willingness that is then confirmed, you are failing the company and creating a void of revenue that takes time to replace. It's all about real-time understanding of progress or lack thereof, ability or lack thereof, and willingness or lack thereof.

Reality check: The major issue here is not one person's sense of entitlement—it's your decision not to develop a strong candidate network and your related decision only to focus on hiring when there is a vacancy. Creating and sustaining an active, engaged network is a critical part of your job description. You should spend not less than 10% of your time networking and recruiting, even if you have zero openings to hire for right now. That figure should ramp up to 25% or even more if you're in rapid-growth mode. Bear in mind that recruiting is a muscle—one that needs to be developed, then maintained. Knee-jerk recruiting that only swings into action when there is an opening ultimately slows you down because it results in bad hires.

"We have met the enemy—and they is us."

–WALT KELLY, AMERICAN CARTOONIST

Key Takeaways

- Saying goodbye to a salesperson who is producing but has entitlement issues accomplishes three important things: it sends the rest of the sales team the critical message that everyone must play by the same rules; it clarifies that it is part of each salesperson's job to function effectively as part of a team; and it clarifies for sales leaders the most critical elements of their own job.
- Your own recruiting, hiring, and management processes are what get you into trouble—not the members of your team.
- Spend no less than 10% of your time networking and recruiting, even if you have zero openings to hire for right now. Build up your network.

Your Commitment

- Share this chapter within your executive committee and discuss the key takeaways.

CHAPTER NINETEEN

"Skate to Where the Puck Is Going"

THIS IS THE FINAL CHAPTER of Part 1. The first part of the book was designed to help you lay the foundation for the Success Cadence for your current team by helping you reach a point of owning your own personal responsibility for your team's performance. By this point, we hope that's where you've landed.

It's time to get ready for the next phase of your team's growth—and your own growth as a sales leader—by exploring the critical takeaways and commitments to turn into regular behaviors in order to create a Success Cadence for your team and your organization.

A quote widely attributed to hockey great Wayne Gretzky is one you may be familiar with: "Skate to where the puck is going to be, not to where it's been."

Too many sales leaders skate to where the puck has been. To cite only the most obvious example of this: They treat recruiting as a reactive task. They focus on recruiting only when they have to fill an opening for a salesperson. When someone important leaves the team, that's when many sales leaders start thinking about who could replace that individual. That's a major blind spot, as we shared in the previous chapter. By now, you know that if you wait until someone you count on leaves to start thinking about recruiting, you're being triggered by a short-term emergency—the fact that there's an empty sales seat you need to fill. If you only focus on recruiting when there's an opening, that means you aren't recruiting and developing talent proactively, on a consistent basis, with the strategic goal of creating a deep talent bench—a reservoir of talent that supports your team's and your company's mid-range and long-term goals.

That's called skating without knowing or caring where the puck is going. It's a lousy way to run a sales team—or a company. It produces nothing but stress.

That stressful approach contrasts sharply with the richer possibility of always being open to building relationships and developing talent, which is what sales leaders who implement the Success Cadence do. In fact, the Success Cadence is impossible without this constant commitment to connect with and recruit salespeople who are willing and able. That means following a process that moves beyond gut instinct.

Changing your current recruiting process means going outside of your current comfort zone. It means you need to keep moving up and to the right. That's definitely worth doing in this case, for the simple reason that talent is the ultimate resource. Don't you really want to attract talent—and retain it—in a way that supports not just where you want to be next week, but where you want your team and your company to be one, two, three, or four years down the line? Don't you want to recruit the very best sales talent from outside the organization strategically—and also to develop your current staff members to be great at their current jobs and their next jobs, based on your future direction?

Make no mistake. That's what skating where the puck is going looks like.

Understand: This is not (just) a human resources responsibility.[*] It's a responsibility for all truly effective sales leaders—and all of those operating at the very highest levels of the company's leadership. After, all, they're the ones who are supposed to know where the puck is going.

> *"Buckle up, and know that it's going to be a tremendous amount of work, but embrace it."*
>
> **–TORY BURCH, FASHION DESIGNER**

Make a Commitment to Develop Talent

Engaging with candidates who can deepen your bench and whose experience and capacities support your team's long-term strategic

---

[*] Too many sales leaders set HR up for failure. HR would be more effective if sales leaders let them in on the business as true partners. For instance, HR can be invaluable when it comes to interviewing for cultural attributes and team fit. They may pick up on important warning signals in these areas that sales leaders miss.

objectives is a critical part of your ongoing job description as a sales leader. It's likely you're not doing this now. If you are not, commit to developing talent on an ongoing basis, starting immediately.

Whenever you meet someone new in a professional setting, you should be asking yourself, "Could this person make a contribution that supports where we want to be five years from now?" Your aim should be to find and develop talented people who will thrive, not just where you are now, but where you are heading.

Creating relationships with new talent on an ongoing basis does two important things. First, it gives you a better answer than you may have right now to the perennial question, "If so-and-so left tomorrow for some reason, what would I do?" Second, it sets your team up for rapid growth in the long term.

Working closely with your executive committee, identify where the puck is going. You will automatically then begin skating towards it. You will create a clear sense of what kind of talent you currently have on staff, which talent is helping you to reach your most important objectives, and whether it will stick around. You should know specifically what experience you want in filling upcoming sales positions—and what the ideal career paths look like for both current and future staff. Remember: The most talented people stick around when they see a clear career path in which they feel confident they can be successful and can make an important contribution as part of something that is bigger than themselves. They are a natural fit for the we-first culture discussed earlier. With this in mind, you should be prepared to create a viable written process for evaluating, recruiting, and hiring candidates who meet the criteria for entry to your team and who can make significant contributions.

In short, you must consider relationship building with new talent your personal priority. Not only that, you must target and nurture the talent within those relationships. Specifically, you must be willing and able to hire people who are better than you. Too many leaders let fear and short-term considerations stop them from making such hires. The willingness to sign people who have skills that you don't is a critical component of a rapid-growth working culture. If you are committed to moving up and to the right over time, you are going to identify weaknesses—voids that need to be filled. Hire people who are better than you are in those areas, so the voids can get filled. This habit of hiring up (rather than hiring down) requires management courage, but it is essential. It is one of the critical drivers of rapid growth.

Stop managing down—and start hiring up. Target and nurture talent. Build up your bench. Specifically, be willing and able to hire people who are better than you.

Recruit and hire to the culture. Recruit and hire to willingness. This is far, far better than hiring on other factors—and then assuming you can convert a new hire to your working culture.

Key Takeaways

- Gut-instinct hiring does not support rapid growth and neither does hiring in which only one person interviews the candidate.
- The most talented people stick around when they see a clear career path in which they feel confident they can be successful and make an important contribution as part of something that is bigger than themselves.
- Rapid growth means hiring talent from companies who are already operating at the level where you want to be two, three, four, or more years from now.

Your Commitments

- Working with your executive committee, create: a) a written job description of your ideal sales hire, including relevant team experience, and b) a first draft of a recruitment process in which at least two highly experienced people must interview, provide written notes on, and concur in the hiring of, any sales candidate. You can refine this job description and this recruitment process later, but create a simple first pass on each right now. Use it in any new hire you make. In setting up these tools, be sure not to over-index on one sales-person's failure. (For a blank willing-and-able matrix worksheet you can use in collaboration with others in your organization to begin the discussion of hiring to the success trajectory, visit www.sandler.com/willing-able-tool.)

- Working with your executive committee, identify all the salespeople on your current staff whom you hope will still be contributing to your organization in any capacity two years from today. Once you have created that list, take each of those individuals out to lunch this month and spend at least two hours discussing that individual's personal goals and aspirations. Do not lecture or attempt to coach these people in any way during these sessions. Spend the entire time learning about them as individuals. Try to identify, for each person, at least one important personal goal that has no direct tie-ins to your corporate goals. (For instance, if your salesperson wants to save up $25,000 for a down payment on a house, that's a personal goal you should know about.) Once you have done that, ask each of these individuals where they see themselves going professionally over the next one to two years.

- Working with your executive committee, identify the annual revenue you would like your company and your sales team to achieve two years from today. Once you have identified this figure, identify at least 10 companies, either inside or outside of your industry, that are currently operating at that higher sales level. Some of these companies may be good targets for your future recruiting efforts.

Do not continue to Part 2 of this book before you have completed all these commitments. Once you complete these commitments, you will be ready to start refining these processes and implementing a customized, calendar-driven Success Cadence for your team.

Part 2:
The Calendar Matters

CHAPTER TWENTY

Your Quarterly Cadence

IN PART 1 OF THIS book, you mastered the core concepts that support the Success Cadence. You got clarity on how the willing-and-able matrix works. You discovered the vital importance of using regular measurements to determine for yourself whether current and prospective team members are moving up and to the right in the most critical areas that connect to their job performance. Finally, you took action to defend your own team's rapid-growth culture to identify and part company with any team members who did not support that culture. We do realize it's possible that everyone on your sales team already fully supported all of the willing-and-able skills and attitudes we shared with you in the earlier chapters as the foundation of the Success Cadence. But we also believe, based on our own experience, that this is highly unlikely. If you are proceeding into this second part of the book without having taken the difficult but essential step of letting at least one me-first salesperson go, understand that what follows is going to be of limited benefit to you.

In Part 2, you will set up a repeating, calendar-driven process that has been proven to deliver aggressive, scalable revenue growth. This is the Success Cadence.

To begin with, you will find out what the Success Cadence looks like on a quarterly and annual scale for your entire sales team. There is a distinct annual rhythm to this—a rhythm that must be understood and implemented before the quarterly and monthly rhythms of the Success Cadence can become operating realities for your team. At its simplest possible level, that rhythm looks like this for the sales leader:

The Sales Leader's Quarterly Deliverables

Q1

- Weeks 1–4: Kickoff, Q1 Reality Check
- Week 4: Face-to-Face with CEO
- Weeks 6–13: Deliver on Q1 Forecast

Q2

- Weeks 1–4: Q2 Reality Check
- Week 4: Face-to-Face with CEO
- Weeks 6–13: Deliver on Q2 Forecast

Q3

- Weeks 1–4: Q3 Reality Check
- Week 4: Face-to-Face with CEO
- Weeks 6–13: Deliver on Q3 Forecast

Q4

- Weeks 1–4: Q4 Reality Check
- Week 4: Face-to-Face with CEO
- Weeks 6–13: Deliver on Q4 Forecast

That's the basic calendar of deliverables that drives you, drives your team, and drives your company. As you might expect, there's a lot more detail to this calendar. We'll be unpacking it for you in much more depth a little later on. For now, here are the basics. The Success Cadence features an annual kickoff event, which is vitally important for team cohesion. After that, the Success Cadence is marked by quarterly reality checks with the team and quarterly face-to-face meetings with your founder/CEO, in which you do a quick look back and commit to delivering certain revenue targets. Each quarter culminates with you and your team delivering on that promise. All of these are critical deliverables for which you are personally responsible.

> *"The way to achieve your own success is to be willing to help somebody else get it first."*
>
> **–IYANLA VANZANT, AUTHOR AND INSPIRATIONAL SPEAKER**

Over the next few chapters, we'll break that down for you in much more detail. You'll get a better sense of exactly what makes such an annual rhythm possible along with what it looks and feels like so that you can implement it successfully within your own team and your own organization. For now, we'll keep it simple. Start with the four quarters of the year in mind, as we've just outlined it, and work to deliver the monthly and weekly outcomes that support those quarterly and annual results.

The calendar matters because time matters. Think of the annual deliverables calendar as being the largest doll in a set of wooden nesting dolls. Inside the big doll is a slightly smaller doll that fits perfectly; inside that doll is a slightly smaller doll that fits perfectly; and so on, down to the very smallest doll. Everything fits; everything is in sync with everything else. This is another way of saying that the annual sales calendar drives what is happening on a daily basis with each member of your sales team.

The calendar matters because when everyone is following the same calendar, information travels effectively in both directions—from the front-line contributor all the way up to the executive level, and vice versa. If the calendar does not support this kind of communication, the data is conflicted and often useless. The implementation of the Success Cadence can start at any level of the organization's selling team, but it must have the buy-in of the senior executive team in order to set the company calendar in a way that delivers company-wide revenue acceleration. The reason for the reality checks you will be doing is for individual contributors to get clear on what needs to happen and what is predictable in terms of their own revenue production this quarter. The reason you are ensuring those reality checks are conducted with every member of every team is so you can all get clear on what needs to happen and what is predictable in terms of each team's production this quarter. The reason you are developing all of those numbers is so that you know what to promise the founder/CEO at your face-to-face meeting—and how to deliver on it.

It all nests together. The way you will deliver on that promise is by living, coaching, and modeling the willing-and-able matrix you learned about in Part 1.

Key Takeaway

- The Success Cadence features an annual kickoff event, which is vitally important for team cohesion. After that, it's marked by quarterly reality checks and quarterly face-to-face meetings with your founder/CEO, in which you commit to delivering certain revenue targets. The quarter culminates with you and your team delivering on that promise.
- Think of the annual deliverables calendar as being the largest doll in a set of nesting dolls. Everything fits; everything is in sync with everything else.

Your Commitment

- Create a first draft of your quarterly calendar.

CHAPTER TWENTY-ONE

The Training and Reinforcement Calendar

WE COME NOW TO THE heart of the system. Your founder, president, CEO, or other senior level executive must understand and sign off on all of the specifics of the training and reinforcement calendar you'll be developing in support of your quarterly deliverables. This is nonnegotiable.

It's important for you to understand that significant preparatory discussions with that senior person will always precede the successful implementation of the Success Cadence for your team. The two of you will be working together to establish both the funding and the political support you need for an annual training and reinforcement plan that drives your sales team and supports rapid, scalable growth.

The key word here is "annual." This annual focus on significant investments in training and reinforcement is mandatory. The sequence and investments of the training and reinforcement that supports your team is something you and the senior leadership of your organization must discuss in depth and must agree on ahead of time. You cannot make the Success Cadence a reality in your organization without investing in a training and reinforcement calendar, and you can't make that calendar a reality without buy-in from the very top.

Of course, the training and reinforcement calendar is different from the deliverables calendar that you saw in the previous chapter. It unfolds during the same timeframe, but it focuses instead on what, specifically, happens over the course of the year to support your salespeople to move up and to the right within the willing-and-able matrix. You will be designing this calendar for your current team in deep collaboration with your senior leadership. Notice that it's a repeating calendar, one that will establish a critical rhythm for your team from this point forward. Take a look.

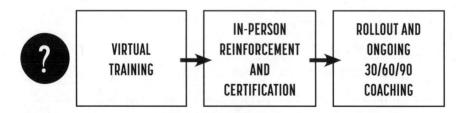

The three boxes in the diagram show the basic priorities for a recently hired salesperson or for a salesperson on staff whom you are considering keeping.

As with the deliverables cadence covered in the previous chapter, this is the simplest possible overview. The most important things to notice about the training and reinforcement plan you'll be designing in collaboration with your executive committee are the following:

- **It all starts with executive commitment.** The question mark you see at the far left is a reminder that this whole process is meaningless unless you and the senior leadership of your organization agree on the answers to some fundamental questions. The answers to those questions will drive everything that happens in the year to come. For the sake of convenience, consider the timeframe in which this conversation about fundamental questions must happen as ASAP. This discussion is what makes everything else possible. You'll learn what the questions are in the next chapter.

- **The training and reinforcement calendar begins with an emphasis on virtual training.** Phase 1 is all about independent learning. You may opt to target, attract, and recruit remote salespeople from today forward. That's up to you, and it's what we recommend. Many leaders find that this approach is the most flexible, affordable, and scalable. Regardless of where your people are working, we recommend that this initial training be something salespeople complete on their own, in a physical environment of their own choosing. You'll learn how to prepare for the training and what goes into it in Chapters 23 and 24. Beginning the year with this intense virtual training session carries a couple of extremely important ongoing advantages: it establishes a pattern of learning and reinforcement that you can continue as necessary for each individual salesperson, based on their personal results as the year moves forward, and it sets up a common playbook and a common language for the team as a whole.

- **The virtual training is followed by Phase 2, an in-person reinforcement and certification session.** This is done in person, at a location of your choosing. You'll learn more about this event in Chapter 25. In-person reinforcement and certification occupies a prominent place in your annual planning for two big reasons:

  1. First, to give you the chance to conduct in-person evaluations and assessments that will give you a clear, measurable sense of where each team member stands in terms of establishing an up-and-to-the-right success trajectory on the willing-and-able matrix.
  2. Second, to instill a sense of shared purpose and team identity. The shared in-person experiences of this gathering are particularly powerful and important for those organizations that opt to develop easily scalable remote sales teams.

- The in-person reinforcement session is followed by Phase 3, the rollout. We've labelled this "Rollout and ongoing 30/60/90 coaching" because that's exactly what happens during this period. This is when your team executes the sales process that generates revenue and supports your quarterly deliverables—and gets ongoing coaching on how to maintain an up-and-to-the-right trajectory. We'll give you more detail about what's happening here in Chapter 26.

This model is endlessly expandable, quarter by quarter, as your team grows. A couple of cautionary words are in order at this point about the critical objective of broadening your talent base. First, in order to scale your growth aggressively using this training and reinforcement calendar, you will, by definition, need to set more aggressive goals and hire more salespeople as time goes on. This means you will also need to start identifying potential leaders on your team who buy into the Success Cadence system and can manage new sales teams. Thus, an important ongoing goal throughout any given year is to spot people with high leadership potential ("HiPOs") who have clearly made the willing-and-able matrix part of their personal long-term growth plan. You must expect to focus on identifying these people and getting them ready for leadership positions within your growing sales team.

Second, it's imperative that there be a good working relationship and high levels of trust between the finance and sales areas. This is nonnegotiable if you plan to ensure consistent, uninterrupted funding for your expanding sales team, for the people who support them in the field, and for the management team to whom they report. This funding should include both hiring new people and promoting existing staff. In the happy event the sales organization is ahead of plan, a working relationship with the finance lead can be leveraged for more funding to hire more people, earlier. On rare occasions, hiring can be slowed down (relative to plan), but note that this creates growth challenges in the near to medium term that tend to compound themselves over time—potentially, for years to come.

It is very hard to catch up with an aggressive income target once your hiring slows down, especially if it takes a long time to get employees to where they are producing optimally or a long sales cycle. The moral here is a simple one: Your sales team's rapid revenue growth, and by extension your organization's rapid revenue growth, depends on you expanding the training and reinforcement calendar to a steadily larger group of qualified new sales hires via an expanding pipeline of applicants. To the extent that you expect the company's revenue to grow aggressively, its applicant pipeline must grow aggressively—and your organization's finance lead must be part of the ongoing plan for growing that pipeline.

> The growth rate of hiring may be less than the growth of your business. Invest in hiring anyway. Bear in mind that following the tenets of the Success Cadence often results in significant productivity increases throughout the organization, not just in sales.

Just as you want linearity—steady, predictable growth, without sudden peaks or valleys—in your company's revenue performance, you want linearity in the expansion of the talent you are recruiting, hiring, training, and reinforcing. Indeed, the two measures are inextricably interlinked in a rapid-growth organization. If hiring gets bunched up in a particular month or quarter, the following bad things are likely to happen:

- The revenue plan may be missed if the management team needs to take its eyes off the business development ball so they can focus on another—namely, recruiting, which has fallen below expectations. They become consumed with making that recruitment number at the expense of managing the existing team effectively. There's no balance.

- Candidates are not thoroughly vetted due to lack of time on the part of those doing the interviews; shortcuts are taken, references aren't checked, and key internal personnel don't plug themselves into the process when they normally would. Why? They simply have too many candidates to consider.
- Up against a deadline, management overpays for sales talent, causing short-term expense issues and longer term morale ones.

Ramping up and then ramping down a process (recruiting, in this case) is like skipping practice on an athletic team for several weeks, and then trying to make it all up on a single weekend. You are not as strong as you would otherwise be, and you are highly vulnerable to injuries. Your onboarding and training/reinforcement cadence (as set out in the calendar model shared in this chapter) is going to be negatively impacted by such an approach. If you create a situation where, during the months of January through September, you have just two people going through the three critical training and reinforcement phases you've just learned about, but then 30 people beginning their virtual training in the first month of Quarter 4, that's grossly inefficient. By suddenly hiring and attempting to onboard 15 times as many people in November as you did for the nine months preceding that, you are all but guaranteeing that those 30 new hires will bury the other functions of the company as they ramp up, upsetting the operating cadence of the entire organization. It's much better to work closely and collaboratively with the finance team on a plan that spreads out hiring a little more evenly throughout the year and then make minor adjustments as needed. If you establish this kind of relationship with your CFO, you are more likely to stay ahead of both your revenue and your recruiting plan, and you will be better positioned to take advantage of situations where other functions end up hiring more slowly than they projected.

What we have shared with you in this chapter is what aggressive scalability for the sales team looks like from 30,000 feet up. This repeatable training and reinforcement calendar shows you what needs to happen in any given quarter in which you bring on new salespeople. It is the heart of the Success Cadence. In the chapters that follow, you'll learn how to make it an operational reality.

Key Takeaway

- Here's what the training and reinforcement that is the heart of the Success Cadence looks like on an annual scale: fundamental questions (now), virtual training (Phase 1), in-person reinforcement and certification (Phase 2), and rollout (Phase 3).

Your Commitment

- Take action. Schedule time now talking with your executive committee in depth about all of this, even though you haven't yet read all the relevant chapters. Ideally, you will want to spend two full days in discussions with this person about the critical content you will be reading about in Chapters 22 through 27, particularly Chapter 22. Since that kind of time may be hard to come by, we recommend you block it off on the calendar now so you can have this vitally important planning meeting as soon as possible.

CHAPTER TWENTY-TWO

The Summit Conference with the CEO

THIS ALL-IMPORTANT ONE- OR TWO-DAY session is represented by the question mark on the far left end of the annual training and reinforcement calendar. That's because there are many important questions to answer.

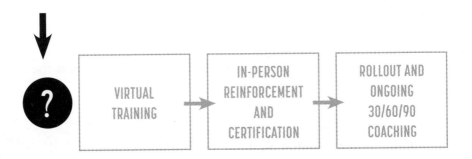

145

We've been talking a lot about having discussions and building alliances within an executive committee—ideally the senior person in your organization. We are assuming you have now established significant rapport with this person, that you are comfortable talking to them, and that you are both on the same page about the importance of developing and executing a rapid-growth plan for your organization. This critical extended discussion between the two of you, the summit conference, is where all of those earlier rapport-building, same-page-identification discussions pay off. This is where the two of you work together to set up a clear battle plan for rapid growth.

Important: You will need at least a full day of your partner's undivided attention, and possibly two days—as well as some significant preparation and research time on your part before this meeting. It's best to think in terms of a working weekend.

The key questions that will come up during your summit conference with the CEO will break down into five specific areas:

- Market questions
- Deliverable questions
- Budget questions
- Timing questions
- Decisions/commitment questions

In this chapter, we'll break down each of these issues and their specific questions in depth for you and the senior person in your organization. The best-case scenario is that you both read this chapter from beginning to end before you hold the summit conference. If you happen to be the senior person in your organization, it's just as essential that you review all of the questions that follow with the person who is in charge of leading your sales team. Note that even if—especially if!—you consider yourself the company's primary salesperson, it is vitally important that there be someone else whose job it is to lead the sales team (as opposed to leading the company, which is your job). Your company's growth will not be scalable if this isn't the case.

Market Questions

You must always start here. The market drives everything. You must begin by looking closely and critically at the current fit for your product or service in the market, and you must explicitly identify the marketplaces where you can expect to add value in the coming year. The main questions that you and your executive committee need to address are:

- **"What typical problems do we solve with our product/ service? For whom? And how, specifically, do we know for sure that we solve those problems?"**

  If you don't solve problems, you don't have a viable business model. It's that simple. Get a clear fix on the *pain*, or the emotional gap between where your ideal customer is before they encounter your company and where you will help them go by working with you. Spend some time on this. Start thinking in terms of the emotionally-driven problems your product/ service makes disappear, instead of in terms of its technical features.* If the two of you don't know where the emotional pain

---

* For more on this important topic, see *Sandler Enterprise Selling* by David Mattson and Brian Sullivan.

is, your sales team won't know either. What business pain does your product solve for the organization or for the person you're talking to? What is the typical financial impact of leaving the problem that your product/service handles unresolved? What challenges do you address on behalf of your key decision makers and their stakeholders? What fear, uncertainty, doubt, worry, anxiety, concern, or anger do you make go away? Who typically feels those negative emotions? How do you know you have made their pain go away? What happens to make it go away? What outcome do you consistently deliver to clients and customers that addresses their pain? For instance: late warehouse deliveries, missed deadlines, and increased turn-over rates among key employees are all examples of emotional pain. Turning each of those situations around is the positive outcome you might deliver. Whatever you do, don't skip this part. Identify the emotions.

- **"Specifically, what measurable outcomes do we deliver to our best clients/customers, such that, if a less expensive competitor came along, they would still choose to work with us?"**

What countable things would your best clients/customers evaluate in making the business case to maintain their relationship with you over time? For instance: How much can you improve on-time deliveries in comparison to your main competitor? By how many days can you shorten production schedules for your clients—without reducing quality? By what number of months or years can you extend the actual tenure of key hires? Get the hard numbers. Buyers don't typically associate a dollar cost to leaving a specific problem unsolved. You should. If you don't know how to make the bulletproof business case for doing business with your company, your sales team won't know either.

- **"How, specifically, have we won our best customers in the past? How have we gotten them to stick around?"**

What is the current process in place for attracting, onboarding, and retaining your customers? What is working for you? What isn't? Proceed from facts, not aspirations. Identify how your best customers were actually brought on board and how they were actually serviced over time. If you don't yet have customers, the stakes get even higher; start by exhaustively researching how your competitors win and hold onto customers and move on to evaluating whether their process is something you can adapt or refine. (We will look more closely at sales process, a central component of virtual training, in Chapter 24.)

Other questions to consider include:

- "What specific value does our firm/product/service create? How does a customer typically describe that value?"
- "How is that value sold, and what does customer success look like?"
- "How does (or can) the compelling value delivered by our product or service connect the dots between what we offer and the vision, mission, and objectives of our customer?"

- "What tools and learning resources for the sales team support that customer success?"
- "Is every ability-related tool and learning resource our salespeople use mapped horizontally for the purpose of reuse?"
- "What roles within our company share the same skills, tools, methods, and processes with our sales team? What resources of the sales team's can they use or adapt?"

Typically, companies create multiple teams that touch the customer, with entirely different tools, resources, and assumptions. As a result, large chunks of customer success are designed vertically, with no knowledge of the sales team's processes, and do not use the same framework, tools, methods, and assumptions the sales team is using. But if all of this is designed consciously by the sales leader, then the process of landing, adopting, expanding, and renewing is easier for everyone (not least, the customer) and the efficiency gains are significant.

- **"How many of our best customers are willing to give us testimonials/case studies?"**

Who has done this in the past? Who could do it in the future? What are the next steps for bringing those testimonials/case studies into existence? What hard numbers (metrics) would make those testimonials/case studies compelling? What next steps will you schedule to make this happen?

- **"How big is the market we are targeting?"**

Start with your most important market; focus on that first. What portion of the market do you possess now? What portion of it do you want to possess, and by when? It is all right if the answers to these questions are in broad strokes initially. You will refine them when you get to the deliverables questions.

- **"Who are the most important competitors in the market, and what are their strengths and weaknesses?"**

Limit yourself to a short list at first. Figure out who should be on your radar screen and why. You can expand the list later.

- **"Last but not least—how strong is our product/market fit?"**

The core elements at play for this discussion are team, product, and market. A team with superb operational discipline (which is, of course, what you are planning to design and expand) can indeed post dramatic revenue growth, given a decent product and a viable market—but it can't deliver scalable growth with a product/service that is unusable or completely out of step with what customers are willing to pay for. So this is a gut-check question, one that continues the earlier discussion about the emotional pain you resolve. Is there a market for the elimination of that pain? How big is that market? How receptive is it? Are people willing to pay good money to make that pain go away? How do you know? Both of you must be certain of the answer to this product/market fit question, and all its relevant follow ups—and you must be willing to stake your careers on that answer.

Deliverable Questions (for Revenue Growth)

When it comes to revenue growth over the next 12 months, who is making a commitment to do what? What are the specific, measurable commitments? What are the financial incentives for attaining them?

- **"What is my revenue target this year as the sales leader?"**

  This is something that must be worked out collaboratively in two directions—between you and the senior executive/founder/CEO with whom you're working today during the summit conference and between you and your team. This may take more than a day to resolve. By definition, this number should be aggressive (you are wanting rapid growth, after all), yet at the same time it should be something that you and your team consider to be a realistic target, both at the individual level and at the departmental level. (See the next bullet; it's important, and it must be taken into account before you finalize your answer to this question.)

- **"How does that revenue goal break down?"**

  Which niches, specifically, are you going to target, and how much revenue are you, the sales leader, accountable for delivering within each? Are your market goals horizontal in nature, or are they aimed at a specific vertical? You may or may not decide to go vertical because your solution may be able to solve pain horizontally—regardless of industry. The decision about whether to target one or more specific verticals is a critical differentiator in itself, one that should not be overlooked or minimized. Begin the process of locking down the numbers, bearing in mind that these numbers will need to be verified from the bottom up as well as from the top down. Too often, a top-down mentality carries the day, and bewilderment follows when the numbers are missed and forensics point to problems that could have and should have been addressed months earlier, via consultative dialogues with the right people. Such problems typically include: not enough ramped-up salespeople, poor product/market fit, under-investment in the right kind of marketing, and poor or non-existent training.

- **"How many additional salespeople will we be hiring, and when, in order to reach this target?"**

Take this question on together. You need to decide whether you are each committed to coming up with a process that expands your roster of sales and sales leadership talent and increases your revenue performance accordingly as you scale. You may decide not to. There's a lot in this book that you can still implement if you decide not to scale in this way—but you must at least have the conversation. A good initial goal might be to expand your sales staff by 20% this year in comparison with the number of salespeople you had on staff last year. Of course, this figure may not be right for your situation, but since this is a book about rapid growth, let us suggest that a 20%

increase in the number of salespeople on your sales staff should be your annual floor, rather than your ceiling. (Note that many companies forget to include likely churn rates in their hiring plans, which is a serious impediment to the rapid-growth culture you're trying to achieve.) Of course, you will need to come up with realistic revenue estimates and timeframes that reflect the hiring levels you are committing to, and those revenue estimates will need to synchronize with your cash flow forecasts. Consider, as you plan, that the sustained absorption of, say, a 50% annual growth rate in the sales organization can result in a whole new set of challenges. These might include: pressures on the customer support/customer enablement team to expand capacity as the sales team expands; pressures on the sales leader to meet hiring targets without compromising quality; pressures on other functions of the business to field and resolve questions from customers and prospects; and on and on. The engine needs to be really humming to support this level of growth, and the margin for error is usually slim in a rapid-growth environment.

- **"What is the right compensation package?"**

You should both be very clear on the details of your own compensation package and the package you will be rolling out with your sales team. Yes, the packages can be altered over time if they need to be adjusted. No, that doesn't mean you should assume your current compensation package is perfect. Note that the beginning of your first Success Cadence year may be the perfect time to launch a new plan that aligns with the goals you and senior leadership formalize today. Be aware that frequent changes to compensation plans, or even to bonus plans aligned to specific products, may cause unintended pauses in sales momentum, as members of the field sales team stop to ponder what the company is asking of them.

- **"How often will you and I be meeting to review my progress on the deliverables?"**

We strongly recommend weekly meetings to review all the relevant metrics. You may opt to make these meetings monthly once you get the program off the ground, but weekly contact is important at the outset.

Budget Questions

What resources are available to you as the sales leader to make all this happen? Specifically:

- **"What is the annual operating budget for the sales department, and how does that break down by expense category and by quarter?"**

You need to get clarity on all the expense categories for the coming year, of course, but two categories in particular are worthy of close discussion during the summit conference.

- Talent development is a priority. How much is allocated to recruiting and training salespeople, based on the calendar commitments that are built into the Success Cadence process? Crunch the real numbers—and make sure you both agree they are realistic.

- Market expansion is also a priority. How much is allocated to securing the specific niches or verticals you identified in the deliverables section? Crunch the real numbers—and make sure you both agree they are realistic.

Important: If you don't make appropriate investments in recruiting salespeople, training/reinforcing salespeople, and penetrating specific markets, you cannot expect to scale rapid sales growth in your organization this year. Again, think horizontally across roles and teams. Think about consciously designing the customer experience, and the tools and touch points that affect that experience. Think about making the process of landing, adopting, expanding, and renewing as seamless and frictionless as possible for everyone—especially the customer. Think, too, about all the personnel who need to be hired to support the sales team. This includes people in management, marketing, customer service/customer enablement, operations, and so on. An unbalanced organization quickly becomes an impediment to rapid growth. As you think about budgeting, think about making synchronization and conscious design of your customer-facing processes an organizational priority—and lead that discussion. You will get economies of scale, and you want to be realistic about those. (Note: You will want to complete reading Chapters 23–27 before you suggest specific budget figures for the coming year.)

Timing Questions

What are the key dates on the calendar? When are the most impor-tant events taking place this year? Specifically:

- **"What are the key events in our annual calendars going to be?"**

  As the sales leader, you should propose the key dates for both the deliverables calendar (see Chapter 20) and the training and reinforcement calendar (see Chapter 21), being sure to sched-ule specific dates and venues for the five most critical in-person events: the all-team kickoff and the four face-to-face commit-ment meetings with your CEO. Important: Note that these commitment meetings must also include your organization's lead finance executive, lead product development person, and lead customer service person, as well as any other members of the leadership team your CEO wants to take part. (Chapters 23, 24, and 25 will give you what you need to know to prepare and execute the kickoff. Chapter 26 will walk you through the rollout. Chapter 27 will give you all the guidance you need on preparing for and leading the critical quarterly commitments.)

- **"When are the key revenue benchmarks going to fall?"**

  These critical deliverables match up with your commit-ment meeting and with the end of each quarter. Mark every-thing on the calendar. We strongly recommend setting both monthly and quarterly revenue benchmarks for discussion and evaluation. Note that you are responsible for delivering these aggregate numbers. The individual members of your sales team are responsible for their behaviors, attitudes, and techniques and for executing their individual behavior plan, but you, the sales leader, are personally responsible for meeting these benchmark dates with the appropriate revenue totals.

Decisions/Commitment Questions

The issue here is a simple one. Will senior management back your play as you implement this plan? If not, there is no point launching the calendar at all.

- **"So to recap—are we saying we are okay with the dates of [X, Y, Z] to launch this, correct?"**

  Replay everything that you have discussed in principle about the Success Cadence annual calendar up to this point. Confirm agreement with it. This is the beginning of the fulfillment phase of your discussion.

- **"Will you support me on this sales team calendar, and on this sales plan, without reservation for the next 12 months?"**

  This is the conclusion of the fulfillment phase of your discussion. It is absolutely imperative that you ask this question and have this conversation. The senior executive/founder/CEO must give you clear, unqualified commitment to support this annual plan. If you don't yet have that support, you must call time out and go back to the drawing board until you both feel completely comfortable making these commitments for the year ahead. The reason this part of the summit conference is nonnegotiable is simple: Other people in the organization are going to disagree with this plan and look for ways to undercut it. They will have a different agenda or a different idea on how to get results, and they will struggle to place their organizational priorities front and center instead of yours. When that happens, and it will, you will need to be able to go to the senior executive/founder/CEO and get their full support. Remember what we said earlier in the book about this being a revolution? About the sales team determining the operational rhythm for the company as a whole? That's always not going to be popular. Some of the people you work with can be expected to say that they agree with what you're doing, but that they only buy into part of the process. They will tell you that they agree with the direction that you're going, but they think you should take the first couple of steps and then everybody should weigh in and reassess what's going on. This approach will kill the Success Cadence before it starts. Don't agree to it.

Your company's CEO/founder must back your play 100% and must agree to continue to back your play over the course of the coming year when conflicts arise (which they will). You will find that you need to sell and resell the key concepts of this system, both to your colleagues in management and to the members of the sales team who report to you because people will be strongly tempted to slip backward into "the way we've always done it." You can't let that happen.

Start every meeting by offering an overview of what you are doing, why you are doing it, and what you expect to see as a result. What you propose must be totally defensible from all angles, must be supported by hard numbers, and must align seamlessly with the company's mission and objectives, as enunciated by the CEO/founder. If you do that part effectively, the part where you align what you're doing with the CEO/founder's most important strategic objectives, you'll find that your forward momentum tends to takes care of itself. (Note that this is also a best practice that your sales team should be deploying with their C-level decision makers.)

- **"Is there anything that would lead you to change your mind about committing to this plan for the year ahead?"**

  Raise this question directly. If there is going to be a problem with rolling out the program, you want to find out about it during the discussion with the senior executive/founder/CEO—not afterward. Even if the CEO doesn't come up with something here, you should. Talk about what you think could derail the plan or cause a slight pivot. What are the leading indicators of these events, and how would your CEO/founder alter the plan if they do? You will build essential credibility and strengthen your working relationship by discussing in advance.

That's what needs to happen during this two-person summit conference. That's what drawing up the battle plan for your revolution is going to look like. This is not something you can wrap up over lunch. It will take extended time commitments. There is going to be a lot of face-to-face work during the summit conference, yes, and also a lot of preparation time on your side that precedes that face time. But it has to happen that way.

Here's one of the biggest reasons this vitally important one-on-one discussion with your CEO/founder is so critical and why it must happen every year, without exception: This discussion mirrors the process you will be asking your sales team to execute in selling your product or service in the marketplace. Think about it.

- They, too, will be **establishing rapport,** setting aside calendar time, and **setting mutually acceptable agendas** with senior people within the organizations they're targeting.
- They, too, will be talking about the **emotional pain (also known as "business pain")** those senior leaders are experiencing, and identifying priorities based on those discussions.
- They, too, will be talking about **budgets.**
- They, too, will clarify the **decision-making process.**
- They, too, will have a clear **fulfillment** conversation based on everything that has gone before, and thereby secure a commitment,
- They, too, will ask directly whether there is **anything that would lead the decision maker to change their mind.** *

Notice that these are the foundations of any and every successful professional sales process. (In fact, the elements we have just outlined combine to form the Sandler Selling System® methodology.)

By covering these bases, in this order, with your own senior leader, you are actually modeling and reinforcing the very steps that will allow the individual members of your team to succeed in their own

---

* As we've noted, the sooner you add the CFO or other lead finance person into the conversation you're having with the CEO/founder, the less likely you are to encounter resistance or reversals about budget priorities.

accounts. You will be sharing those steps with them, along with many other things, during the next phase of the Success Cadence calendar: virtual training.

Key Takeaway

- The summit conference is a critical one-on-one meeting between the sales leader and the senior executive/founder/CEO that addresses important questions about the market, the deliverables, the budget, the timing, and the commitments for the coming year. If the budget includes revenue targets, those should be highlighted.

Your Commitment

- Keep reading. Move forward to Chapter 23, which is about preparing for virtual training.
- Finish reading Chapters 23–27 before you hold your next one-on-one discussion with the CEO/founder.

CHAPTER TWENTY-THREE

Preparing for Virtual Training

WE COME NOW TO THE task of getting yourself and your team ready for the period of intensive, vigorously monitored virtual training of your sales team—a training session that will be followed, in the next phase, by an equally vigorous session of in-person assessment and

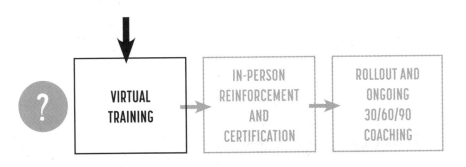

163

reinforcement. It's important to understand that these two events are interconnected. There's zero reason to do the one without the other.

Virtual training typically requires 10 calendar days. Some companies will not need that long; others may need a little bit longer. In the final analysis, what matters is not the number of days you spend on this, but whether the team can execute your sales process and use the resources you have prepared for them. If you think of the people on your team members of a hockey team, virtual training is what gets them ready to take the ice.

We emphasize this extended virtual training phase because the most dramatic and most scalable pattern for rapid growth that we've seen is the model where the sales team takes part in an intensive self-paced learning regimen for multiple days. They should do this under their own steam and in their own chosen location, using the tools and resources the sales leader has put together, and operating under the guidance and supervision—via email, phone, and video conferencing—of that sales leader: you.

Once virtual training is complete, the salespeople then gather with the entire team to meet with you at a central location of your choosing for the next phase, in-person reinforcement and certification. Their goal there will be simple: to prove to you beyond a shadow of a doubt that they can apply in the real world what they've learned from you at a distance.

A great deal of preparation goes into making these two phases pay off for your organization. In this chapter, we will be looking closely at what must happen ahead of time in order for both phases to succeed. We'll look at the virtual training in the next chapter.

Welcome to Phase 1

During your first pass through the Success Cadence calendar, you will focus on training (or retraining) people who are currently on staff as well as training any recent new hires in the same fundamentals. Obviously, if you are starting from scratch with all new hires, you won't have any current staff to lead through this training. Regardless of which path you find yourself following, everyone who reports to you as a salesperson must be prepared to go through the two phases of virtual training and in-person reinforcement and certification, whether the individual in question is a recent hire or a new one.

There should be a sense of focus, urgency and, most notably, high personal stakes—a sense of getting ready for a big event (namely, reinforcement and certification) that will confirm a person's right to stay on as a member of the team. The stakes are, in fact, high. You as the sales leader must make it clear to everyone that the right to sell for the team is indeed contingent upon the successful completion and reinforcement of virtual training. This training should be positioned as the equivalent of a bar exam for an attorney or a medical licensing examination for a physician. If someone cannot pass the test virtually and then in-person in a hands-on environment, how can you possibly expect that person to sell to a live prospect or expand an existing business relationship? Why wouldn't you require such vigor when your stakeholders are counting on you to grow the organization aggressively?

It is also worth pointing out that sales hires who are unwilling or unable to complete a 10-day remote program of self-paced learning are probably also incapable of working effectively without your close daily personal supervision. That's not a scalable team. This is a critical point to take into account—especially if you tempted even for even a moment to skip or alter the virtual training phase.

You don't want a team of people who require close supervision. You want self-governing teams, teams populated by self-starters who are supremely focused and goal-oriented. These first 10 days on the calendar are where you will begin determining whether that's what you actually have. If you have the right talent, they will not only complete the training, but also help you to improve it over time. The 10 days of virtual training are thus vitally important days, days that are worth preparing for. Most of the preparation will be on your side, and much of it will involve changing the way you think about recruitment and onboarding.

> *"I always did something I was a little not ready*
> *to do. I think that's how you learn."*
>
> **—MARISSA MAYER, AMERICAN INFORMATION TECHNOLOGY EXECUTIVE**

The Five Pieces of the Puzzle

Who should be receiving this intensive training and reinforcement in the first place? After all, the first two phases of the Success Cadence calendar represent a significant investment of your time, your attention, and your company's resources. We need to look critically at how people even get to this spot on your calendar—and specifically at the puzzle pieces you will be assembling in order to put them there.

Recall that the product you supply as sales leader is salespeople who are both willing and able to do their job.

Recall, too, that your goal is to scale—that is, to predictably expand—a sales team that's capable of delivering aggressive revenue growth.

It follows from these two points that you (and any managers who may report to you) must accept the need to be in constant search mode for new sales talent.

That means you must make attracting, training, and retaining new salespeople who are both willing and able to make a significant revenue contribution to your organization an ongoing personal and organizational priority. Just as you expect salespeople to hold themselves to the standard of maintaining a funnel of qualified prospects, you must hold yourself to the standard of maintaining a funnel of qualified sales candidates.

Like a sales funnel, this funnel must be replenished regularly. Given the astronomically high costs of a bad sales hire you will want to vet the most promising people rigorously before enrolling them in the virtual training phase. It's possible that some of your colleagues or even your CEO/founder will be skeptical about the actual costs of a poor sales hire. Be prepared to share your sources on this.

- According to "The True Cost of a Bad Hire—It's More Than You Think" (Forbes, September 28, 2016), the actual cost of onboarding a single employee, when all the direct and indirect costs are taken into account, is estimated at $240,000. The same article quotes Zappos founder Tony Hsieh as saying that bad hires cost his organization "well over $100 million."
- In her book *The Right Hire,* author Lisette Howlett estimates the true cost of a bad sales hire at between 10 and 25 times the

person's annual salary, once you figure in onboarding, support, and lost opportunity costs.

- "The Best Ways to Hire Salespeople" (Harvard Business Review, November 2, 2015) points out that in such sectors as medical devices, capital equipment, and professional services, including all the support and opportunity costs of a bad sales hire pushes the true cost to "$1 million or more per event."

The best available information all points in the same direction: a bad sales hire is a catastrophic outcome. When you ask for the recruitment resources necessary to do the job right, make it clear that what you are really asking for is support in avoiding that catastrophic outcome.

Recruitment should be a recurring, expected part of your role as a sales leader—not something you only think about when there is an empty seat to fill. Generating a pool of qualified hires to support this year's growth targets and initiating relationships with people who can support next year's growth targets is always going to be part of your job.*

Make no mistake: It is your recruiting/hiring process that will be tested during the virtual training phase—and it is your recruiting/hiring process that will ultimately determine whether the Success Cadence delivers positive results for your organization.

This is what makes a Success Cadence leader different from everyone else who leads a sales team. You must accept that your own

---

* A corollary of this is that you will make attracting and retaining the support staff whose work is essential to the success of those salespeople a personal priority, too. For the sake of clarity and simplicity, we're focusing on the salespeople in these chapters, but you should understand that administrative staff and technical support teams need to be part of your hiring and retention plan, too—as are new managers to oversee new sales teams.

success or failure within your role and the success or failure of your sales team depends on your ability to consistently assemble these five puzzle pieces:

1. Be in search mode for new talent.
2. Bring new willing-and-able salespeople into the organization in a way that is scalable and supports your revenue goals.
3. Onboard those people effectively.
4. Confirm that they were in fact the right hires to make (and part company if they turn out not to be).
5. Get the right hires to stick around and grow as the company grows.

All five of these pieces of the puzzle are necessary for a successful launch of Year 1. All five are interrelated, although many sales organizations fail to grasp this fact. To understand how these five puzzle pieces interconnect and why they must all come together in order for you to conduct a successful virtual training, look at some common but critical misconceptions that many leaders have about the much-misunderstood business of onboarding salespeople.

Three Common Misconceptions about Onboarding Salespeople

The first misconception is that onboarding pretty much takes care of itself—if you hire the "right" person or team the "right" person up with an established performer who can serve as a role model. Many leaders tell us, "We only hire experienced people. They don't need onboarding." That's simply false. No one is that experienced. It's fine to have peer role models, but this is no replacement for a good onboarding experience. Even the best hire needs a clear playbook, specific performance benchmarks on the calendar, and strong management support in the early going. This is particularly true of sales hires, on whom so much depends.

The second misunderstanding is that effective onboarding starts once the person officially reports for work. There are vitally important onboarding issues that must be taken into account with the most qualified candidates during the interview process itself. Just as you expect your sales team to qualify a prospective customer before the sale is considered closed, there are multiple qualifying issues that you must address with a promising sales candidate—issues that set up, overlap with, and support the onboarding experience that salesperson will eventually have if they are hired. To put it most simply: The relationship with the company starts during the interview process— which means an important element of the onboarding has begun then, too. If you are recruiting top talent and you cannot explain exactly how you plan to make the person successful by ramping them into your working environment, someone else will—and you will lose the person to the competition.

The third, and perhaps most dangerous, misconception is that onboarding is primarily for the employee. Ultimately, onboarding is about giving you, the sales leader, the data that you need to decide whether it makes good business sense for you to retain a given sales hire. If it makes sound business sense, based on the benchmarks this person has posted, to hold onto this person, the person has passed probation successfully. If it doesn't make sound business sense, you will part company, It's that simple. And yes, this standard does apply to people on your current sales team who don't do well in virtual training and reinforcement. Indeed, it should apply to everyone in the organization.

Consider: Some of the people you hire (or have hired) will make truly dramatic positive contributions over the 30, 60, or 90 days that follow virtual training. Others, alas, will not. Some of the people in that second group will demonstrate to you by means of their performance that they are not in the right job. This is a fact of management life. So: Which group would you rather hold onto? And just as importantly, when would you like to know who falls into which group?

Strategically speaking, the whole point of your onboarding process—the virtual training phase, the in-person reinforcement and certification phase, and the first 30–60 days of the rollout phase that follow those two phases—is to show you clearly and quickly who is delivering on your significant investment in making a sales hire and who isn't justifying that investment. Your aim as sales leader is to use the data arising from these critical weeks to make a strategically sound Go/No-Go decision about whether it really makes sense to hold onto a given salesperson. If it doesn't make sense, you want to find that out a month or two in—not after a year or two. (By the way, what we're focusing on for sales hires in these examples applies equally to technical ones and even hires from other functions.)

Tic-Tac-Toe vs. Chess

A few moments ago, we told you that the onboarding process actually starts during the interview process with your best prospective sales candidates. Did you feel yourself pushing back at that notion?

It's common for people to be surprised and maybe even little skeptical when they hear that for the first time. We want to explain now why and how this can be so, and why the content of the discussions you have with prospective salespeople during interviews has such a major impact on your ability to conduct and reinforce a successful virtual training session with them.

Many sales managers think of a job interview with a prospective candidate as being like a game of tic-tac-toe: simple, basically two-dimensional, and strategically limited to a simple question: "Can this vacancy be filled quickly?"

Recall that when sales leaders are hiring only to fill a vacancy (which is what typically happens in most organizations), they're usually in emergency mode. In order to get out of that mode, they end up treating the hiring process like a simple checklist, one with three boxes that can be filled and set aside relatively quickly:

- They talk to a number of candidates so they can eventually run into someone they have a good feeling about.
- If feeling ambitious, they ask for a professional reference. (Many managers skip or abbreviate even this step, which is inexcusable, given the relative ease of securing a formal or informal reference on a candidate.)
- If the reference checks out, they hire what they pray is the right candidate, thereby filling the vacant seat.

Tic-tac-toe, three in a row—done. Emergency mode is over. Now they can forget about hiring for a while and get back to what they think, incorrectly, is their real job—micromanaging the team and putting out its many fires. If the salesperson that was just hired doesn't work out, well, that's the way it goes sometimes. They'll play the same simple three-step game all over again as the need arises.

This tic-tac-toe recruitment game is a guarantee for slow or non-existent revenue growth—and a downward spiral for the sales leader and the company as a whole.

The reason the tic-tac-toe approach to hiring salespeople doesn't work is that it doesn't support your actual role as the sales leader. Your goal is not to micromanage the sales team or to swoop in like a super-hero to save the day when something goes wrong. Your job is to grow sales teams that are composed entirely of people who are capable of addressing most day-to-day issues on their own and who don't need (or want) Superman or Captain Marvel to materialize every other day to fix the latest problem. The best way to grow such a team is to hire it in the first place. Tic-tac-toe doesn't get that job done. It can't.

What we're talking about—and what needs to happen to make your virtual training successful in both the short and long terms—is something much more strategic in nature, something much closer to the game of chess.

What we're talking about here is a recruitment and hiring process that employs patience, careful planning based on your team's growth objectives, and long-term strategic thinking in at least five different areas—all of which are essential if you are serious about getting the right people into, and through, your virtual training session. Those five areas are:

- Screening out your own bias.
- Screening out the candidate's possible entitlement issues.

- Using the willing-and-able matrix to drive the emerging relationship.
- Establishing alignment in both the short and long term.
- Networking.

Let's look at each of these now.

Chess Move 1: Screen Out Bias

Have you ever found yourself thinking something like the following? "This person seems like a good bet. In fact, they kind of remind me of myself at that early stage of my career. I'm going to follow my gut and give them a shot. I know talent when I see it. I don't need to talk to anyone else." Or: "This process has taken forever—they're good enough, so let's make the offer!"

We've already mentioned this in an earlier chapter, but the point is vital enough not only to repeat, but to lead this list: There must be no more gut instinct hires and no more hires based on interviews that only you conduct.

You must get at least two other people, ideally three or more people, involved in the interview process. If you don't have that many in your own team, then look outside to marketing, HR, or a functional executive with experience in hiring to help out and give you another data point. The decision does not need to be unanimous. You are just trying to get to the truth about what you're "buying," and you have a better chance of doing so with these inputs. Yes, it's your job to bring sales talent into the organization. It's also your job to get good feedback before you do. It's your job to make sure you are following a clear process, so your team knows what to ask and what to look for. When you make a decision to hire someone, that hire represents a significant investment of company resources—an investment that reflects directly on you. Do not make that decision without input and due consultation with others in your organization.

Failing to ask others to interview promising candidates dramatically increases the odds that you will favor a certain kind of candidate, one who matches your own communication style or who reminds you, for reasons you can't quite clarify, of some other salesperson you like—perhaps yourself. This bias, which may be based on superficial factors, leads to unbalanced and underperforming teams that require constant care and feeding. Again, that's not scalable.

To avoid biased hiring decisions, you need a clear, written set of hiring requirements that each candidate must fulfill in order to be seriously considered for the job. These requirements should, at a minimum, take the following SEARCH elements into account:

- **Skills**—Identify the most important skills necessary to perform at a high level within this role. For example, a proven ability to begin business conversations with C-level decision makers.
- **Experience**—Describe the specific experience base you are looking for within this position. For instance, two years of personal experience selling to your #1 target industry.
- **Attitude**—Quantify an applicant's ability to bounce back from failures, stay focused on goals, remain positive, and sustain a healthy self-concept. There should be zero entitlement issues. (See Chess Move 2, which deals with this specifically.)
- **Results**—Quantify actual sales figures this person should have

delivered in previous jobs. Past performance is an indicator of future results. What have they actually accomplished? If you don't know, you will not be able to create achievable performance metrics.

- **Cognitive ability**—Identify the mental and logical processes the new hire should be able to employ in order to succeed rapidly within this role. What kinds of problems should this person be able to solve? What kinds of planning—internally and externally—do you expect this person to take on? Be as specific as you can. Look for evidence of the kind of cognitive ability you are looking for in the person's job history.

- **Habits**—What everyday work habits are required to support success within this role? For example, how many conversations with decision makers should occur each day? How many are with current clients? How many are with brand new business prospects? What business development activities need to take place? What evidence is there in the applicant's work history that they have sustained this kind of habitual approach to the job of selling? How do they approach the week, month, and year? Do they have a plan? What are they proud of as their own best practices?

(For a blank SEARCH worksheet you can use in your hiring and recruiting process, visit www.sandler.com/SEARCH-tool.)

The halo effect—the common practice of hiring based on a candidate's perceived similarities to another successful salesperson or, even worse, to yourself—can kill your team's potential. By looking closely and objectively at all six of the SEARCH criteria, by using those criteria to formalize your hiring template in writing, and by involving others whose opinions you respect in the interview process and checking for appropriate references, you can go a long way toward screening out your own personal bias. Another great tool for this is a well-designed behavioral assessment.

Remember that you really will need to seek input from at least one or two (ideally three or more) trusted voices within your organization (or other functions) on whether the person you are considering hiring hits the mark in all six of these areas. Their detailed written input should be based on personal discussions with the candidate. In the event that there is a toss-up between two equally qualified candidates, you can take your gut instinct into account—but that's the only time "it just feels right" should come into play.

The higher the pay and the quota of the position, the more people you want involved in the recruitment and hiring process. Think about it. If you're going to be paying $300,000 a year for a salesperson, that's a major organizational investment. Wouldn't you want at least four or five people to evaluate the candidate before you make the hire? Shouldn't those people come from a variety of different places within the organization? Getting cross-executive buy-in before such a major investment is good for your team—and good for the applicant.

Note that while it is your responsibility to seek out the opinions of others, the hiring decision itself is yours and only yours to make. As your organization expands, you will hold managers who report to you to this same standard. They, too, will be evaluated by the level of talent they choose to bring into the organization.

Chess Move 2: Screen Out Entitlement Issues

We've talked a lot about the danger of a sense of entitlement in earlier pages, and yes, we're going to be talking about it again here—for one very important reason: You will never have to worry about replacing an unwilling-and-able salesperson if you don't hire that salesperson in the first place.

Never forget that an able salesperson who expects to play by different rules than everyone else on your team is, by definition, unwilling to support the values and the culture of your team. The hiring and retention of such salespeople is the single biggest obstacle to sustaining a rapid-growth culture on your team. Salespeople with entitlement issues make an aggressive growth curve an impossibility. So, this is the second chess move you must master.

People with entitlement issues are sometimes very good at camouflaging their attitudes during job interview sessions, which presents a major problem for sales leaders. We're often asked whether there is a single simple way to identify and screen out sales applicants during the initial interview so that you don't end up investing lots of time and energy on multiple discussions with a candidate who doesn't really belong on your team. Fortunately, there is such a tactic. During the initial interview, ask some variation on the following question:

You: Can you describe from your time in your current company [or "a company you worked for in the past"] a situation where you were pursuing an advancement, a particular territory, or a new role, and even though management knew who you were and what your performance record was, you had to put some effort into proving you were ready for the move?

This behavioral interview question is a highly reliable detector of an entitlement mentality. Time after time, you will find that people who operate from a we-first mentality—a "we" mentality, rather than a "me" mentality—will answer with something like this:

Applicant: Sure. I was very eager to move up to [role/territory/advancement], but I found that I had to work closely with [mentor/colleague/other teams/workgroups/senior management] in order to make it happen. It turned out there was a lot for me to learn, much more than I imagined. I got a lot of support and encouragement along the way from [name].

Those may not be the exact words of course, but you get the idea. The we-first sales applicant will go out of their way to identify the specific people and teams who were helpful in securing their career goal. It's quite common for these people to single out a mentor who was particularly helpful and to make a point of heaping praise upon that person. This is exactly what you want to hear. This is a sign that you should keep talking to this person.

What you will hear when you're dealing with an applicant who has entitlement issues sounds very different. The entitled response will be something like this:

Applicant: I had already earned that promotion [or whatever it is]. I had worked hard, and I deserved it. Really, it was a gimme.

You: Really? Tell me more about why you felt that way.

Applicant: Well, I'd been there for two whole years—

This kind of exchange is not what you want to hear.

If you encounter any variation on this in response to the question we've just shared with you, know that this candidate is not right for you. This is someone with a me-first mindset, an entitlement mindset. It's highly unlikely this salesperson will ever adopt the we-first mentality necessary for your team to succeed at a high level, support each other, and scale revenue growth aggressively. Do not make a job offer to this person.[*]

Here are some additional questions you can use to determine whether and how well a candidate fits with your organization's sales culture and process:

- **"Tell me about end-of-quarter and how you approach it or how your leader approached it in the past."** If you hear stories about a lot of personal heroics, discounting, and save-the-day behavior to meet quota at the end of the quarter, those are all red flags. If the candidate considers the end-of-quarter period a non-event, one that solid planning and predictability render more or less identical with any other time of the year, that's a good sign. A combination of the two approaches means you're dealing with someone who falls in the middle of the spectrum.
- **If they mention making a discount to get a sale to close by a certain date: "Tell me more about the discount."** Follow ups

---

[*]   For more on the vitally important topic of hiring and retention, see Lisette Howlett's book, *The Right Hire.*

include: "What happens if the sale does not close? Do they still get the discount? What is the value you created? Why would you then discount?"

- **"Tell me when you had to tell a customer [internal or external] 'no,' and how you handled that situation."** A good sign here would be a decision to say "no" because of a risk to the business or the possibility of compromising integrity. Follow ups include: "So what happened?" You're looking for some variation on: "I provided the following options that were acceptable and fair..."

- **"Tell me about a time when you faced adversity and how you handled that."** A very revealing question. Follow ups include: "What did you do? What did you learn from that? Did you seek guidance from anyone?" If the instant answer to that last follow up is "no" accompanied by a tart expression, consider that a red flag.

- **"What is your preferred sales process?"** With this question, you are trying to discover whether the candidate has a sales process or prefers to fly by the seat of the pants. Seat of the pants is not good! The answer you receive should tell you whether this person has the discipline to stick to something that works; whether they will buy into your sales process; and whether they know enough about sales to describe in detail how a sales process and a buyer's journey map together. The candidate does not have to be an expert at your sales process, but should be flexible and knowledgeable enough to adapt to it. If the candidate is experienced and can't describe a sales process or prefers not to follow one, run away. If hired, this person will become a lone wolf and will inhibit your organization's ability to scale. On the other hand, if the candidate is fresh out of college or has never worked in sales before but exhibits a willingness to follow your process, the lack of familiarity with a specific sales process should not be a disqualifying factor.

- **"What was your first job?"** Ideally, you're looking for answers that point toward proactivity and personal initiative: "I delivered papers," or "I sold books door to door," or "I worked in a call center for a non-profit organization."

- **"When is the right time to bring someone else into a selling situation?"** Any indication that the candidate views this as a worst-case scenario or as something to be avoided altogether constitutes a red flag.

- **"Have you ever found yourself in a situation where someone else got involved in a selling situation and the deal then fell apart? What happened?"** If the candidate instantly moves into "victim" mode here, and shows no sign of learning from the situation or of having come up with a better way of handling the same kind of issue the next time around, it's likely there are entitlement issues.

- **"We all get screwed occasionally, if we're in sales long enough. When did that happen to you?"** If the candidate says it's never happened, it's possible the person hasn't been in sales very long, in which case you may want to reword the question to explore a time when the candidate felt management was unfair or hasty. In the far more likely eventuality that the candidate says there was such an event, your job here is to check on tone and body language and notice whether the person assumes some level of responsibility for what happened—or decides to play the blame game.

- **"Who influenced you most while growing up and why? What traits did you like about that person?"** These questions give you a good sense of the person's formative influences.

- **"During your professional career, who have you looked up to? Why?"** The answer should give insight into the candidate's ethics and other professional attributes. When they mention the names, you can also probe deeper about what the candidate considers those leaders' specific good or bad behaviors to be.

- **"CEOs, as we know, make a lot of money. What is the appropriate ratio of their pay to the lowest contributor's pay?"** Here, you're looking for their understanding of the principles of pay for performance, responsibility, and value delivery. There is no specific right answer.

- **"What personality trait do you observe at work that irritates you the most?"** You're looking for a response like, "I don't really pay attention to that kind of thing because I have too much work to do." Other responses give you good opportunities to probe deeper into how well or poorly this person might fit into your culture.

Chess Move 3: Use the Willing-and-Able Matrix

You'll recall this matrix from Chapter 14:

The Success Cadence^{SM} WILLING-AND-ABLE MATRIX

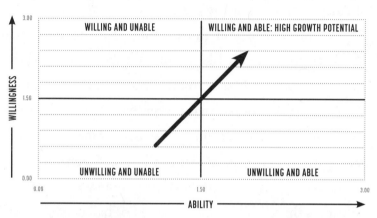

Is This Person Willing?
(Behavior & Attitude)

- Desire
- Drive
- Coachability
- Possibility mindset
  (as opposed to scarcity mindset)
- Company focus
- Team focus
- No entitlement mindset

Is This Person Able?
(Technique & Application)

Skills will vary by specific position, but basic skills always include:

- Strong communication, both internal and external
- Executes a documentable sales process
- Negotiation skills, both internal and external
- Sets and defends Up-Front Contract, bonding and rapport
- Analytics (monitor and track personal activity with measurable daily, weekly, quarterly outcomes)
- Customer and business acumen

The candidate who makes the first cut and has managed to convince you that they merit serious consideration to become (or remain) a member of your team needs to see and understand this matrix during the interview process.

The willing-and-able matrix needs to become the basis of the candidate's entire relationship with you, with the team, and with the company. Also, the candidate needs to understand clearly that the whole purpose of the virtual training period they will take part in, if hired, will be to confirm the employment decision by ensuring that there is an up-and-to-the-right direction in everything that's measured with this matrix. A parallel discussion needs to happen one-on-one with each member of the current sales staff. Everyone must understand and buy into the idea that monthly and quarterly coaching sessions will then be taking place to ensure that the up-and-to-the-right dynamic continues in a measurable way over time. The playing field is level for everyone. Everything is based on willingness and ability. It's not personal. It's about performance, as trained and reinforced.

Use this matrix to clarify exactly what the job is and also how performance within the job will be measured over time. Confirm that the person is comfortable being assessed and coached on all the "willing" components and all the "able" components you've adopted for your team—not just once, but on an ongoing basis.

Suppose there is pushback. Suppose the candidate (or the employee) shows signs of hanging onto a habit of not following through on commitments to discuss the daily and weekly behavioral plan during coaching sessions or filing the attendant activity reports—e.g., how many discussions took place, with whom, and where those discussions left the opportunity in your sales process. What then? Simple. You will not offer to bring the person on board or keep the person on board.

The willing-and-able matrix is the starting point of all your performance-focused conversations with all promising applicants—and with all salespeople you hire or decide to retain. Both you and the salesperson must accept this matrix as a central element of your working relationship and the foundation of the virtual training.

An observation about current members of the sales team is in order here. You'll recall that in an earlier chapter, we advised you to hire well and fire better. That principle becomes even more important as you prepare for virtual training. While hiring well, based on a profile that aligns with the willing-and-able matrix you've set up for this specific job, is indeed crucial, firing better is an equally critical management skill—one that becomes more important as your organization grows. No hiring and recruitment process is perfect. When you do make a mistake—and you will—that mistake must be rectified quickly, and it must also be rectified with care, dignity, and grace.

A lot of this depends on simply being honest with yourself. Most of the time you know very quickly when a hiring mistake has been made. The longer you wait to fix that mistake, the more difficult the moment of truth is going to be for both parties, especially if performance is suffering. Success Cadence sales leaders know how to part ways quickly and with little or no drama. If they can help the person to find a job that's a better fit, they do. Regardless of whether that's possible, they respect the other person's dignity throughout the termination process for two reasons: first, because it's the right thing to do, and second, because they know that this person's experience of them as a leader will inevitably affect the company's brand, in the pool of potential hires and everywhere else.

Chess Move 4: Establish Alignment, Both Short- and Long-Term

To win in the game of chess, you must think at least two to three moves ahead. (Grandmasters can somehow think 10 to 15 moves ahead.) The same principle applies to the people you target, recruit, interview, and bring on board to your sales team. You're not interested in just the short-term question of whether this person can make an aggressive revenue contribution over the next 3 to 6 to 12 months—although that is important.. You're also interested in what this person's ideal career path is over the next three to five years. Because you're interested in that, you're going to make a point of discussing the subject in depth during the interview process with your most qualified candidates. (You will also want to repeat this same process in one-on-one conversations with the members of your current sales team, if you haven't already done so.)

Please understand that we're not just talking about asking, "Where do you see yourself in five years?"; jotting down the answer; and then moving on to another question. We're talking about a much, much deeper conversation, a conversation in which you establish true alignment between the team's goals and this person's personal goals over the next three years, at a minimum. This conversation should enable you to understand what is going on in their world to make this job make sense over that span of time, and it should ensure that you each have clear, explicit, and realistic expectations about what those three years are likely to look like for both sides from a financial point of view.

"You take your life in your own hands, and what
happens? A terrible thing: no one to blame."

—ERICA JONG, AMERICAN AUTHOR

We're talking about a job interview that uncovers not just the fact that this person wants to earn, say, $250,000 over the next 12 months, but also the personal reason that the person wants to earn that much. For instance: "I want to put a down payment on my dream house this year, and I want to create a college fund for my daughter of $300,000 that will be ready for her to draw down on within the next five years." Ideally, you want to get that kind of openness and that kind of specificity. The beauty of this kind of questioning is that you can use it to help the candidate or existing employee back into the behaviors that must occur in order to achieve those earnings. This becomes a working plan over time. The ability to inspire and collaborate on such a plan is a critical leadership skill.

Most of the managers we meet with have never come close to having this kind of conversation with their current team members, much less incorporated such a conversation into their interview process with the most promising sales candidates. They're used to hiring in response to immediate vacancies so they commit to a cursory discussion, at best, of the candidate's personal motivations and long-term career objectives.

Here are three important reasons for you to avoid that pattern.

First and foremost, having a deeper conversation about the person's personal and financial goals will improve your retention numbers with the most qualified people. Whether you're talking about brand-new hires or the seasoned performers who are already making a major contribution to your team, you are going to be flying blind as a manager if you don't know what motivates the individual salesperson to bring a certain revenue total into reality. Simply sharing the corporate goal with the person tells you nothing about their level of personal buy-in to that goal.

On the other hand, you will learn a great deal about what's driving that individual when you ask, "Just out of curiosity, if you were to hit your target of X, what would you do with the money?" Simply having that conversation and making it clear that you're committed to helping the person hit the goals necessary to buy that dream house and put their daughter through college (or whatever the goal is) will increase the chances that a top performer will stick around for the long haul. That's a big part of your growth strategy: getting top performers to stick around.

Second, the strong personal bond you create will improve the possibility that you can secure additional employment leads from this person. We'll cover this eventuality in depth in just a moment, in Chess Move 5.

Third, talking about where the person is now and where they hope to go will help you spot emerging managerial talent. Remember that you are hiring to support aggressive, scalable growth. That means you are looking, not just for high-potential salespeople, but also high-potential management personnel. So, for instance, in your interview with candidate Lydia, you notice that she has a strong SEARCH profile, a strong cultural match with your organization, zero entitlement, and a background that not only matches up well with your hiring template for salespeople but also matches up fairly well with your profile for future sales leadership. She used to lead a customer service team, and she was successful in that role. If everything else lines up, why not hire Lydia to fill the role of salesperson for, say, the next 12 to 18 months and then position her on a learning and development path that allows her to step into the role of manager of her own team when she's ready to make that move?

Wouldn't you rather have someone ready internally to fill that slot when the time comes? Wouldn't it be good to hire Lydia knowing that you're both working toward such a goal? Not everyone will fall into this category, of course, but it's your responsibility to find the people who do so you can make a seamless battlefield promotion when it's time to launch a new team and to select their ideal manager. Cautionary note: It's important not to commit to a future position, as things change rapidly in rapid-growth mode. Making a promise you don't keep can lead to poor morale and even a poor reputation in the marketplace if the person subsequently leaves because of an unfulfilled commitment. It is much better to talk about the possibilities that come with growing the business together and how shared efforts open doors that would not be opened otherwise. If you and your company establish a reputation for positive employee movement, that reputation will spread through the A-list grapevine, making recruiting easier.

Chess Move 5: Networking

Because you are in constant search mode, you will want to use the personal networks of highly qualified sales candidates, as well the networks of your current sales team, to develop contacts with new prospective hires. Don't just think about Year 1. Think about Year 2 and beyond.

Your search for talent is technically endless, just as your sales team's search for revenue is technically endless. In the same way that your team's sales process needs to incorporate a strategy for generating referrals for new business, you as the sales leader must leverage your personal relationships with highly qualified applicants and your relationships with your own high-performing salespeople to identify new talent that you can bring into the organization. Whenever you identify someone who has potential, remind yourself that birds of a feather really do tend to flock together. Make a point of asking that person who else they would recommend as a potential sales hire for your team.

These relationships may not turn into immediate hires, but immediate hires are not the only thing you're focused on. Your job is to create a deep base of talent from which you can draw so you can grow the sales team over time.

In hypergrowth, it's best if you have a sales leader who can be versatile in the strategies used to build and expand the team, drawing some from their own network, some from new blood off the street, and some by developing existing personnel. In this way, you'll energize and diversify the thinking and culture of the company while preserving the good that is already in place. In the end, this gives you the best chance of creating an enduring organization.

Now What?

In this chapter, we've challenged you to prepare yourself and your team for the all-important virtual training session by broadening the way you look at your role as a leader. We've encouraged you to see yourself as being in a constant search mode for new sales talent; as being personally responsible for targeting and bringing new willing-and-able sales talent into the organization on an ongoing basis; and as being responsible for confirming that the members of your current sales team really are willing and able. With that new vision of your job in mind, you now have the basic tools you need to ensure that the right people are in place for your virtual training session. In the next chapter, you will look at what they must learn in those critical 10 days.

Key Takeaway

- The whole point of your onboarding process—the virtual training phase, the in-person reinforcement and certification phase, and the first 30 to 60 days of the rollout phase that follows those two phases—is to show you clearly and quickly who is delivering on your significant investment in making the hire and who isn't justifying that investment.
- You will never have to worry about replacing an unwilling-and-able salesperson if you don't hire that salesperson in the first place.
- The willing-and-able matrix needs to become the basis of the sales candidate's entire relationship with you, with the team, and with the company. The same goes for all the current members of your sales team.

Your Commitment

- Create a first draft of your first-round interview questions.

CHAPTER TWENTY-FOUR

Virtual Training

AT THIS POINT, WE ARE going to assume that you are confident with the proposition that the people you've recently hired as well as the people you decided to give the chance to stay on staff are the right people. We're going to assume that you have a good sense of who does and who doesn't belong on your team. Now the question is: How do you make absolutely sure those people are all playing from

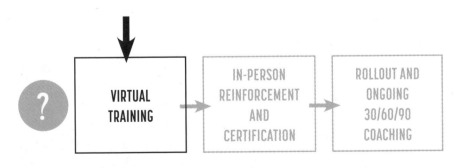

the same playbook? How, for that matter, do you make sure they are all familiar with and comfortable with the playbook?

The answer lies in the mission-critical phase we call *virtual training*. This is something everyone on or about to join your team needs to do once. It's something they must do in order to begin the process of securing or retaining a position on your team, something that prepares them for the "show us you can actually do this" experience they will encounter during the upcoming reinforcement and certification event. Again, think of successful virtual training as being equivalent to studying effectively for a bar exam or a medical exam; think of the reinforcement and certification event as being equivalent to passing that exam.

Virtual training doesn't work without two things: the willing-and-able matrix we've already shared with you (customized appropriately to your selling environment) and an online asset that we call a *safe zone*. Let's look briefly at how each of those things support the virtual training experience.

The willing-and-able matrix. You'll recall that we advised you to share the willing-and-able matrix with prospective sales hires during the interview process. Before the prospective team member even begins the virtual training phase, they should:

- **Be familiar** with exactly what is tracked on your company's customized willing-and-able matrix. So, for instance, one of the "willing" elements of the matrix is a willingness to adopt a team focus. Your salesperson should know that and be able to discuss what that means to them. Similarly, one of the "able" elements of the matrix is the ability to set and defend an up-front contract. Your salesperson should at least know what that is and be able to discuss it. (If the person hasn't yet been trained, you can't necessarily expect them to set an up-front contract, but a basic familiarity with the concept is essential.)

- **Understand leading and lagging indicators.** Discussions about the "able" component of the willing-and-able matrix—the skills part—will focus relentlessly on leading indicators, as opposed to lagging indicators. Most sales teams focus on lagging indicators: what has closed recently or is about to close. On a Success Cadence team, however, the most important discussions in terms of pipeline management are all about the measurable activity that leads up to something closing. Why? Because before there is a "how come nothing's closing" problem, there is always a "how come there's not enough activity" problem, a problem with the level of activity generating qualified prospects or advancing the sales process. Activity is a leading indicator. Getting a commission is a lagging indicator. This is a critical distinction for the salesperson and the manager alike. Whenever we talk with salespeople about metrics that drive personal and team revenue, we're always going to be focusing on the activity that initiates prospect relationships and moves those relationships forward. So, for example, if part of your sales process involves launching initial voice-to-voice conversations with CFOs, the salesperson needs to know that the number of those conversations is going to be tracked and evaluated on a consistent basis as part of the "able" half of the willing-and-able discussion.

- **Accept that there will be regular coaching sessions** based on the latest metrics for every element identified on the willing-and-able matrix. In other words, to be part of this team is to be prepared to be coached on the willing-and-able matrix and on the best ways to sustain a success trajectory within it. Specifically, that means being ready to be coached on everything you see below.

The Success Cadence℠ WILLING-AND-ABLE MATRIX

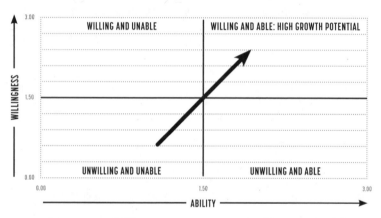

Is This Person Willing?
(Behavior & Attitude)

- Desire
- Drive
- Coachability
- Possibility mindset
  (as opposed to scarcity mindset)
- Company focus
- Team focus
- No entitlement mindset

Is This Person Able?
(Technique & Application)

Skills will vary by specific position, but basic skills always include:

- Strong communication, both internal and external
- Executes a documentable sales process
- Negotiation skills, both internal and external
- Sets and defends Up-Front Contract, bonding and rapport
- Analytics (monitor and track personal activity with measurable daily, weekly, quarterly outcomes)
- Customer and business acumen

All of this is nonnegotiable. If the salesperson hasn't grasped the importance of being personally familiar with the willing-and-able matrix, of distinguishing leading from lagging indicators, and of being coachable, that person is not yet ready for virtual training. All of those issues should be covered in voice-to-voice interactions with you, or with another leader on your team, ideally during the interview process.

The safe zone. This is a virtual environment where those who are learning your organization's selling methodology can study your sales process, complete exercises you design to help them practice their skills, use the tools you've created for them, and (eventually) create deliverables for real customer engagements. This environment can be as bare-bones or as robust as your budget and your schedule permits. At the far end of the scale, you can use a commercially available project management software package or even enlist your IT team's help to design a custom online environment exclusively for your team. If you don't have the resources for that, you can simply set up a folder on Egnyte, Google Drive, or other platforms, grant incoming members of the team access to it, and store your resources there. The key considerations are that the safe zone be accessible to both you and the salesperson, comprehensible at a glance, and easy to update.

What to Put in the Safe Zone

Now for the next big question: What should you put in the safe zone? This will, of course, vary from company to company, but the bare minimum is outlined below.

Your Team's Customized Willing-and-Able Matrix

This should incorporate all the basic elements we've shared with you, as well as any specific measurables that are unique to your sales process and market. For instance, if launching initial voice-to-voice conversations with CFOs shows up as a critical part of your sales team's sales process, that should be added as one of the items you track on the "able" axis. Beware of crowding the matrix with too many elements; keep in mind that you will be measuring and discussing each element in both the "willing" and "able" categories as part of your coaching sessions with each salesperson.

A personal version of this matrix, one that identifies exactly what the new hire's performance will be measured on and includes the new hire's name, should be available as well. By the end of virtual training, the salesperson must understand what's on the matrix and why—and be able to discuss it without having to look at it.

Your Team's Sales Process

Document what actually happens to turn a contact into a customer. Lay it out in a way that your very best salespeople vouch for (and follow); lay it out in a way that a new salesperson can understand and eventually replicate. Pay particular attention to the critical question of what causes an opportunity to move forward from one category of your system to the next. For instance, if you're selling complex software solutions that require a champion at the prospect company to collaborate in detail with your salesperson on the specifics of the solution before that solution is presented, make sure the process diagram reflects that.

Here again is a simplified breakdown of the Sandler Selling System, which should serve as the foundation of any customized sales process you develop for the safe zone.

- **Establish rapport** and **set mutually acceptable agendas** with senior people within the organizations you're targeting.
- Talk about the **emotional pain** those senior leaders are experiencing, and identify priorities based on those discussions.*
- Talk about **budgets.**
- Clarify the **decision-making process.**
- Have a clear **fulfillment** conversation based on everything that has gone before, and thereby secure a commitment.
- Ask directly whether there is **anything that would lead the decision maker to change their mind.**

"Selling is what takes place when you lead the prospect through a step-by-step process, each step of which may lead to the prospect's disqualification and removal from the process. If you do not disqualify the prospect opportunity, the sale moves forward and eventually culminates in the prospect making a buying decision."

—DAVID SANDLER, FOUNDER OF SANDLER TRAINING

Virtual training should make it absolutely clear to your new hire that their real job is to disqualify opportunities so they can spend their precious time with the people who are truly qualified.

The Answer to the Question, "What Do You Guys Do?"

When you were talking everything over with your CEO/founder,

---

* Emotional pain is rooted in business pain. For instance, constant inventory shortages are a function of a poor inventory management system; this can result in the emotional pain associated with losing an important customer because of stock shortages—and perhaps losing one's job as well.

you got clarity about the specific business problems resulting in emotional pain that typically causes someone to enter into a serious discussion about buying from you. The safe zone should include your team's best, most accessible answer to that question, from the point of view of the prospective customer who is actually experiencing the pain.

This is not the kind of answer most teams deliver. Most salespeople, when asked what they do, offer an answer that comes from the organization's perspective. What they say in response to "What do you guys do?" sounds something like this:

> We are a full-service accounting firm that has been around for over four decades. We do state and federal taxes, and we also offer retirement planning and other financial services for both businesses and individuals. By providing a unique mix of resources, experience, and expertise, we partner with our clients to provide the best solutions at the best prices.

Notice that this common response does nothing whatsoever to engage the listener on an emotional level. Now consider a response like the following, based on the actual emotional discomfort connected to the problems your organization solves:

> We are an accounting firm that assists companies and individuals to eliminate the unknown when it comes to managing their finances. Often, our clients came to us because they were worried about losing hard-earned money—in some cases, more than $250,000—because they were unsure of which tax breaks were available to them. Others feared not having enough money put away for retirement and were frustrated about what to

do next. We help our clients deal with similar financial concerns. Is any of that relatable for you?

Your safe zone should give the salesperson a draft of this second kind of "worried/unsure/feared/frustrated" response—also known as a 30-Second Commercial—to customize and practice out loud. Notice that it includes a hard-currency estimate of the solution experienced by an actual client: cutting the tax bill by over $250,000, legally. There should be one such commercial for each discrete market you are asking the salesperson to target, along with a brief description of that market, an overview of its initial target contacts and decision makers, and an explanation of why you're pursuing that market. It's a good idea to include the specifics of a business case narrative that makes it easy for the salesperson to understand how and to whom your company has actually delivered content, as well as any relevant endorsements and happy customer lists the salesperson may benefit from using. Initial training is not complete if the salesperson does not establish mastery over this content.

Here is an example of a typical, unengaging answer to the question "What do you guys do?" that you might hear from someone selling a software solution:

> We are a software-as-a-service company that has been around for five years. We are focused on improving operational capabilities, allowing you to deliver services faster by providing a unique mix of workflows for delivering applications and services securely and efficiently.

And here's a more compelling 30-second commercial for the very same company crafted by a high-tech sales leader committed to the Success Cadence:

> We are a software-as-a-service company that is changing the way customers deliver revenue generating applications, typically making them 30–50% faster, allowing them to decrease time to market and increase revenue, while at the same time reducing compliance and external risk exposure by 60–70% compared to a more traditional approach. Most executive buyers use our platform to change the way they pursue digital transformation to improve agility, reduce costs, increase revenues, and reduce risk within their teams and companies alike. We typically find this aligns more closely with their corporate initiatives than the traditional approach and does a better job of overcoming business and technical roadblocks that are preventing mission-critical outcomes. Is any of that on your radar screen?

Important: The language of your team's 30-second commercials—and indeed all the language of all the promotional material associated with your team's products and services—needs to come directly from the experience and insights of the sales team. It's quite common for marketing people, with the very best of intentions, to try to dictate this kind of messaging to prospects and customers. That's a mistake. Let the sales team take the lead on messaging. If there's a problem with this, appeal to your executive committee.

Training in Specific Selling Tools and Processes

Your goal here is to provide all the remote learning modules, tools, and resources your team needs to master the following behaviors:

1. **Lead generation:** Prospecting, the #1 behavior that drives all the others.

2. **Building relationships:** Establishing a strong, open relationship based on trust.

3. **Making the business case and following through.** Identifying the personal and organizational pain, setting benchmarks for the proof of value leading up to the sale, and then creating alliances that ensure value realization after the sale. (LAER— Land, Adopt, Expand, Renew—is not possible if the customer does not experience value from the first purchase.)

4. **Qualifying opportunity:** Determining a reason to do business.

5. **Making presentations:** Presenting solutions to the prospect's problems.

6. **Servicing customers:** Delivering superior customer satisfaction.

7. **Account management:** Maximizing business in each account.

8. **Territory development:** Building a strategy to grow the territory.

9. **Building a Cookbook for Success:** Establishing productive sales activity via a daily and weekly activity cadence.

10. **Continuous education:** Developing ongoing product, market, and sales knowledge.

11. **Execution of the system:** Mastering the defined, documented sales process.

Full disclosure: This is a lot of work. You may opt to set up a relationship with a training partner to create these resources, but that's certainly not mandatory. The tools and resources you provide to support the learning modules that train these 10 critical behaviors may include, but aren't limited to: referral generation strategies, common talking points for specific markets, customizable calling scripts and email templates for specific markets, articles that can help move prospecting conversations forward in specific markets, and any sample forms, documents, and presentations you feel the person should be ready to discuss and use. The basic principle: If you want the person to be able to execute it at reinforcement and certification, make sure they have the training and the supporting tools they need to execute it during virtual training.

> You may choose to work with a training partner in setting up the core components of the virtual training program. For some ideas on cutting-edge remote training options you can build into your virtual training curriculum, check out shop.sandler.com/online-courses/sandler-microlearning-collection-sales-system.

During the virtual training period, it's your organization's job to help the salesperson get deep familiarity with all the tools and processes that you know for certain, from past experience, will be needed in the specific markets and situations that the salesperson will be facing. Ensuring they know when and how to use specific resources—and, just as important, when not to—is the team sales leader's responsibility. Make sure it happens.

The Virtual Training Benchmarks and Sandler's Cookbook for Success

Set up the specific expectations you have for this person, and make sure they are timeline-driven. For instance, by the end of Day 2, you might choose to have the salesperson be ready to role-play delivering the 30-second commercials for the three different markets they will be targeting; by the end of Day 4, to be ready to role-play a basic prospecting call in each of those markets; and by the end of Day 6, to be able to deliver a mock presentation based on a specific scenario you create. All of this can be done via Skype or another conferencing platform of your choice. You could then set the expectation that the salesperson begin initial live prospecting outreach on Days 7–10, tracking all relevant activity. Important: Focus primarily on activity (the leading indicator), not on closes (the lagging indicator) when you ask your salesperson to go live during the initial training phase.

The culmination of this careful benchmarking process is for both of you to evaluate the results collaboratively during the final days of virtual training and then use the data to come up with a first-draft Cookbook for Success that will outline what the salesperson's daily and weekly activity targets should look like. This should go in the safe zone as well. It will become a formal activity cadence that the salesperson commits to during reinforcement and certification. The cadence will be refined quarterly, by means of ongoing coaching.

"So often people are working hard at the wrong thing. Working on the right thing is probably more important than working hard."

–CATERINA FAKE, AMERICAN ENTREPRENEUR

Save the Training in Specific Products for Later

Note that product training only happens after sales execution and operational discipline skills have been mastered and the salesperson has completed both virtual training and reinforcement and certification. Never teach features and functions first. Without an understanding of the business pain that drives the sales cycle, features and functions are worse than useless. If others have problems with this approach, appeal to the executive committee.

Check In by Phone or Videoconference Once a Day

The leader of the sales team should have at least one individual voice-to-voice or face-to-face interaction with salespeople who are in virtual training each and every day. Keep the lines of communication open!

Key Takeaways

- Virtual training is there to make sure each member of your team is comfortable with the tools they will be using and the playbook they will be following.
- What the salesperson learns and reinforces during virtual training they will execute, in person, during the kickoff in order to confirm their place on your team.

Your Commitment

- Set up a virtual training plan that covers all the points discussed in this chapter. (You may need to work with a training partner.)

CHAPTER TWENTY-FIVE

Reinforcement and Certification

THE DAYS OF VIRTUAL TRAINING have set the stage for an up-and-to-the-right trajectory for each participating salesperson. Now, at the in-person reinforcement and certification event, your job is to determine whether there is proof of concept of that success trajectory among those who took part in virtual training.

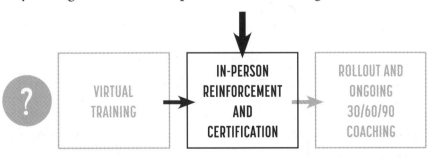

This is your event—the event at which your prospective sales hires become your formal sales hires. By the time this event concludes, people will have either passed their probationary period or failed to do so. The assessments, interviews, group exercises, and role-plays you conduct over this four-day "boot camp" will determine who falls into which group. Those who pass will be people who are working full time as contributors at your organization, reporting (directly or indirectly) to you. This event is therefore, for all practical purposes, the point in the year when things begin to get real. It's the point at which people begin working in earnest, under your leadership, to fulfill the strategic objectives set by your executive committee. You will be their role model, which is as it should be.

It makes sense, then, to take another close look at the willing-and-able matrix. This time, though, we will be looking, not at its requirements for the sales team, but at its requirements for you, the sales leader. It is during reinforcement and certification that you will begin to put the Success Cadence into active collaboration—not with just any team, but with a team you have persuasive reason to believe is composed entirely of people who are both willing and able. This critical period is where you will begin to demonstrate, in person, that you, too, are willing and able to do your job—a job that is very different from that of a front-line sales contributor. We'll be looking at your willing-and-able matrix for the simple reason that this matrix is what will be driving all the most important activities of these critical days— and indeed the performance of the entire team in the year ahead.

Your personal commitment to excellence must spark the team's commitment to excellence.

*"Be a yardstick of quality. Some people aren't used to
an environment where excellence is expected."*

—STEVE JOBS, AMERICAN BUSINESS LEADER

Your Own Success Trajectory Drives the Team's

Earlier in the book, we asked you to look closely at these questions: "What kind of person are you looking for? What traits does the ideal sales hire always possess, no matter what industry you're in or what your market looks like?" In order for you to plan and execute a successful kickoff, you must now ask the same questions of yourself. Your capacity to do this, now and over time, will ultimately determine the trajectory of your team and your organization.

- What kind of leader do you have to be to make all of this work?
- What traits must you possess, regardless of what industry you are in or what your market looks like?

The answers here are just as clear—and you must commit to live those answers, in person, every day, if you expect your reinforcement and certification event, and your team, to be successful.

You must be able to model all of the abilities you expect from the members of your sales team—but notice that your job is not to close sales. It is to target, attract, and retain salespeople who are willing and able to do the job of selling. So your ability requirements go a good deal deeper.

Make no mistake. It is your personal success trajectory that will drive this event. If you are on an up-and-to-the-right trajectory, the people who pass muster will launch aggressive revenue growth for your organization. If you aren't, they won't. It's that simple.

Your Abilities

Your reinforcement and certification boot camp and your entire year must be driven by your ability to do several things.

1. **Translate the message from the boardroom all the way to the individual salesperson; train all levels of management to do the same.**

Use an early session to share the mission, the vision, and the strategic goals of the coming year. Make sure these objectives align with what you have worked out with your executive committee.

2. **Identify, hire, and develop sales talent using the willing-and-able matrix.**

You began doing this, of course, before the virtual training phase even began. You will now consolidate and continue the process over these critical days by making sure that each and every salesperson who completed virtual training completes one or more private one-on-one assessment sessions. These sessions must confirm the salesperson's ability to:

- Identify the markets being targeted, as well as the likely titles of initial contacts and decision makers. This discussion is the payoff of all the resources and one-on-one connections you built into virtual training. If the salesperson chose not to take advantage of all that and can't discuss this without looking at a computer screen, they are not ready to work for your organization.

- Discuss, in terms that will cause the prospect to lean in, the value that your organization brings to each market. These are the 30-second commercials we looked at in Chapter 24. They should sound authentic, comfortable, and spontaneous as the salesperson delivers them in their own words. They should not be looking at a screen as these words are delivered.

- Describe and be totally comfortable with the various steps of your sales process. This is vitally important. Everyone on your team must describe the process using the same steps, and no one on staff should have to look at written prompts in order to describe it.

- Engage effectively in real-time role-playing, using written scenarios you create that are based on real-life selling situations. The scenarios must be realistic and must reflect specific challenges your salesperson will face in interactions with live prospects. It's best if you play the buyer and other trainees play supporting roles. Use these role-play sessions to determine the salesperson's ability to traverse all the typical stages of the sales cycle, and deploy learnings and resources accordingly. (For instance, the salesperson should be able to customize a 30-second commercial to appeal to a specific decision maker.) This part of reinforcement and certification will not only tell you about the salesperson's ability to use the tools, processes, and messaging learned during virtual training, but will also give you invaluable insights as to the salesperson's coachability.

- Describe and be totally comfortable with what their personal willing-and-able matrix looks like. The salesperson should be able to summarize all the "willing" elements and all the "able" elements in their matrix, including key metrics that are specific to your team, such as, "Launch initial conversations with CFOs within the target market at agreed-upon levels." If the person can't do this without checking their notes, they are not yet ready to work for your organization.

Creating private, face-to-face sessions in which you confirm that you have identified, hired, and are now developing the right sales talent is the key deliverable of reinforcement and certification. This is the point where you formally execute on your responsibility to identify and hire salespeople who are willing and able. Make sure it happens!

3. Build short-term, medium-term, and long-term pipelines, using all resources effectively.

You will do this by creating a personal, one-on-one agreement on the weekly, monthly, and quarterly cadence that your salesperson is committing to, based on the *activity cadence* (another name for the Cookbook for Success) you both put together collaboratively during virtual training. It's a good idea to make this agreement a signed document. Such an activity cadence should feature daily and weekly activity targets, not closing targets. The daily activity cadence template you work out with each salesperson during reinforcement and certification might look like the accompanying chart.

DAILY ACTIVITY CADENCE

Name:

Activity	Goal	Actual	% of Goal
30-Second Commercials communicated to C-level decision makers via email, physical letter mailed, or physical letter hand-delivered			
30-Second Commercials communicated to C-level decision makers via voice-to-voice contact			
Requests for introduction to new contacts via contact with LinkedIn connections			
Requests for introduction to new contacts via other sources (such as calls to current clients or calls made on your behalf)			
Networking touches online (such as: webinar delivery-generating contacts or posting an article that generates new contacts)			
Initial appointments booked (in person or virtual)			
Follow-up appointments booked (in person or virtual)			
Net new contacts made			
Net new opportunities created (next step in place)			

The activity column on the left is something that will vary by company and by industry, of course. What goes into the goal column depends on what you and your salesperson work out together—and what they are willing to commit to making a daily priority. Note that "net new contacts made" and "net new opportunities created" are critical leading indicators of pipeline development. Don't just measure closed sales. Measure these indicators, too.

Five daily cadences deliver the salesperson's weekly activity cadence, which in turn gives you weekly and monthly data from which to extract revenue estimates. Will the activity numbers ever need to be tweaked? Of course. That's what your check-ins and coaching sessions will determine. For now, understand that the kickoff is where you get a formal commitment, ideally written and signed, from each salesperson to commit to a certain specific daily and weekly activity cadence.

The activity cadence is the engine that drives your revenue-generation machine. If the two of you get this right and maintain the engine properly, all things are possible on both the organizational and the personal level. If you don't get this right, there's the possibility for missed opportunity—and lots of drama. Revenue is better than drama. Get a clear agreement on the daily and weekly activity cadence and on the principle that predictability is better than heroics at the end of the quarter. Certification is not complete unless you get this agreement, in person, from each and every salesperson.

A side note: The salesperson's activity cadence is your single most important resource in building short-, medium-, and long-term pipelines—but it is not the only resource. Other resources you are responsible for leveraging include support from the executive committee, Finance, Marketing, your product team, Operations, and other sources within the organization. That means you must sustain pragmatic, productive, fact-based relationships with all of these teams.

4. Focus on analytics.

This means you have the same skill in tracking and measuring critical activities and outcomes that you expect from the members of your sales team. In your case, though, it also means you use numbers to lead. You remain measured, fair, and unemotional in the face of facts, and you never succumb to the temptation to yell at the scoreboard. Maintain this kind of analytics focus during your one-on-one meetings with each salesperson. Always focus on the numbers, on the activity—and never on the drama. Here are three principles that will help both you and the salesperson to maintain an analytics focus, both during the reinforcement and certification boot camp and going forward:

- **Manage the behaviors.** Salespeople can't control the amount of sales they will close. Those numbers belong to the prospects and customers, not to your team. What the team can control is their own behaviors.
- **You can't manage anything you can't control.** Too much behavior will cause burnout. Too little will cause failure. In order to strike the right balance, use the activity cadence as your behavior program. Review it regularly and adapt it over time as necessary.
- **The bottom line of professional selling is going to the bank.** Your salesperson must know what, specifically, has to happen

in order to go to the bank and meet their obligations. How this person gets paid—via a draw, salary, 100% commission, or salary plus commission—really doesn't matter. How long the selling cycle is, whether it's a one-call close involving a single decision maker or a two-year purchasing process involving dozens of people, doesn't matter either. What matters is doing the right activity cadence every week—so the salesperson can go to the bank.

The "big idea" behind the team analytics focus is to make the sales-person—and the sales team—self-governing. The principle here is simple: "If my behavior is correct, I work for myself. If not, I work for my manager." You want people and teams who work for themselves. Other skills to master:

- **Look around the corner and plan for the future, so you can communicate accurately and effectively about what's happening—and what's about to happen.** What you learn about the activity cadences you set up with individual salespeople will begin to tell you what the income picture is looking like. Gather all the relevant data during reinforcement and certification. Start connecting the dots. Begin getting a sense of what the team is capable of—so you can engage in accurate planning and forecasting, for both the salesperson and the executive committee.

- **Build and sustain a lean organization.** A lean organization is one that places a heavy cultural emphasis on access and has minimal staff jobs. A lean organization forces innovation and quick decision making. No matter how big your organization eventually gets, it needs to respect person-to-person communication within and between departments and functions over the creation of layers of bureaucracy. Make this point explicitly during reinforcement and certification by emphasizing your personal availability to your direct reports after boot camp concludes and by supporting the cultural values of innovation and quick decision making.

- **Spot and eliminate inefficiencies.** Send the clear message that your team is about the relentless pursuit of productivity in all phases of operation. Let those who make the cut by being certified for a full-time position with your team know that they are among the elite. Let them know that it's your job to maintain a keen eye for the financial and organizational implications of every single hire and that you hired them because you felt you could count on their help. Ask for their support in spotting and addressing any organizational obstacles they encounter along the way. Promise them you will take action to clear the way for them. Keep that promise.

- **Drive accountability in every role and function.** The members of the sales team must leave the reinforcement and certification phase certain that there is no place to hide. That may sound harsh, but the phrasing is important to understand and repeat to your team. "No place to hide" means that, by choosing to work on your team, they have chosen a working culture that demands and rewards transparency. "No place to hide" means that everyone makes a difference, that everyone moves the needle, and that there are consequences up and down the chain of command for each and every decision. Let them know that you'll be communicating frankly about all that. Everyone you certify should understand on a personal level that there is now a clear commitment to sustain a success trajectory by fulfilling the daily activity cadence you've both agreed on. They should understand that, as the sales leader, you will support them—and hold them accountable—to ensure that they meet that commitment. They should also understand that cross-functional selling is going to be a requirement. There will be situations where they will need to be comfortable with a team-selling model and comfortable working side-by-side with technical and service people. This is a core accountability.

- **Identify and support HiPOs.** HiPOs are high-potential employees—people with the potential to make leadership contributions beyond the dimensions of their current job description. Identifying such individuals is an important part of your job and an essential requirement of a rapid-growth culture. Reinforcement and certification is a great place to start looking for and flagging HiPOs—the next generation of leadership. If you aren't developing new management talent, then, by definition, you aren't pulling your weight as a leader in a rapid-growth environment. (You will learn more about this in Chapter 27.) HiPOs are the cream of the crop. They consistently and naturally show up in the upper-right quadrant of the willing-and-able matrix, based not on wishes or predictions but on actual performance. That's just where they live. They are totally focused on helping other people.

- **Create and support a learning culture.** This begins, of course, with the virtual training phase, but it must continue here—and it must continue throughout the year. Markets change; products change; priorities change. The reinforcement and certification boot camp you've used to capitalize on virtual training should be followed by quarterly one-on-one coaching sessions—learning tracks that continue the ongoing task of refining and expanding your inventory of virtual learnings and tools. Note once again that this long-term training and reinforcement must be budgeted. A rapid-growth culture is impossible without investing in learning.

In addition to setting up learning tracks for your sales team, you will also want to set up quarterly learning tracks for HiPO sales management candidates who are making the transition to leadership roles and for anyone else who has management responsibility—including you. We call this a *leadership academy*.

Those, then, are the nonnegotiable elements of the "able" portion of your willing-and-able matrix. The specifics of your company, your industry, and your market will give you other elements to track in terms of abilities (skills), but start with what we've shared above.

> *"Failure is not the opposite of success, it's part of success."*
> **–ARIANNA HUFFINGTON, CO-FOUNDER OF HUFFPOST**

Your Willingness

The success of your reinforcement and certification boot camp also depends on your ability to fulfill the key willingness requirements of the sales leader's willing-and-able matrix. Let's take a look at those now.

Your reinforcement and certification boot camp and your entire year must be driven by your willingness to:

- **Model and support a we-first working culture.** This begins, of course, with you adopting, as your personal daily standards, all of the "willing" elements you expect to see from your team: desire, drive, the possibility mindset, and a team/company focus that excludes any form of entitlement. But it doesn't end there. You must walk the walk, not just talk the talk, by prominently and visibly putting the team and the company first— not just during reinforcement and certification, but on every day following. In short: Do what you know is right. Do the right thing when everyone is looking and also when no one is looking. Do the right thing when no one will even know. This is known as the high-road mentality, and it is nonnegotiable in sales leaders.

- **Think like a stakeholder.** An important part of your partnership with the founder/CEO, and anyone else on the executive committee is a commitment to view the implications of your decisions through the lens of people such as customers, stockholders, and members of the board of directors. Make this responsibility of yours clear to each and every one of your salespeople during your one-on-one meetings and also during group events.

- **Think long-term.** Short-term outcomes are important and must be clearly understood—but scalability is all about creating a selling organization that is built to last. Land this point with everyone on your team, specifically with the people you are welcoming on board as full-time employees during your one-on-ones. Let them each know, once again, what you first let them know during the interview process: that you want to collaborate with them in building a career, not just a sales job. If you do what's right for the long term—in terms of contracts, customer relationships, systems, processes, and everything else—managing short-term outcomes actually becomes much easier. You are putting out future fires now by extinguishing the smoldering embers before they flare up.

- **Pick your battles.** Specifically, disengage from all personal drama. This is a critical cultural value of a rapid-growth organization, so be prepared to show your team how it's done. If a potential conflict situation arises during reinforcement and certification (or at any other time), play it smart. Do your level best to move the discussion to a one-on-one setting rather than a group setting. Don't make it personal. Never, ever humiliate anyone in front of others. Once you're one-on-one, take a deep breath, get some perspective, and decide for yourself whether this fight is really worth fighting. It may not be. If it is, take the high ground and do not yield it. Focus not on your organizational or political authority, but on what best supports the mission, vision, and objectives of the company.

- **Set your ego aside.** When in doubt, give the credit to other people. While not all great salespeople can do this, all great sales leaders can and must.

Sales leaders, too, have a success trajectory. Your personal willing-and-able matrix, which appears below, is a roadmap to a successful kickoff event. Take a look—and then use this chapter and your own customized matrix to design and execute a great kickoff.

The Success Cadence^SM WILLING-AND-ABLE MATRIX for Leaders

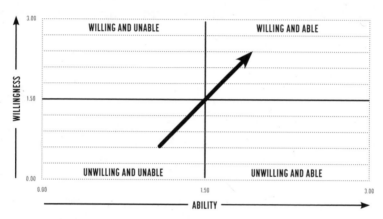

Are You Willing?
(Behavior & Attitude; includes Salesperson's WILLING elements and...)

- Model and support a "we-based" working culture
- Think like a stakeholder
- Think in the long term
- Pick your battles
- Set ego aside

Are You Able?
(Technique & Application; includes Salesperson's ABLE elements and...)

Skills will vary by specific position, but basic skills always include:

- Identify, hire, and develop sales talent using willing-and-able matrix
- Build short-, medium-, and long-term pipelines, using all resources effectively
- Team analytics (monitor and track team activity with measurable daily, weekly, quarterly outcomes)
- Look around the corner/plan for the future/ communicate about future outcomes
- Build and sustain a lean organization
- Spot and eliminate inefficiencies
- Drive accountability in every role and function
- Identify and support "HiPOs"
- Create and support an ongoing learning culture

Key Takeaways

- The multiday reinforcement and certification boot camp event ensures that what people learned during virtual training can be executed, in person, face-to-face. Those who execute what they've learned and create a personal agreement with you about their daily and weekly activity cadence confirm their place on your team.

- Leaders, like salespeople, have the potential for a success trajectory that is based on fulfillment of the requirements of their personal willing-and-able matrix.

- Your personal willing-and-able matrix, when combined with the guidance in this chapter, is your roadmap to a successful reinforcement and certification event.

Your Commitment

- Set up a boot camp plan that covers all the points discussed in this chapter. (You may decide it makes sense to reach out to a professional training partner to do this.)

CHAPTER TWENTY-SIX

Rollout and Ongoing 30/60/90 Coaching

IF YOU HAVE SET EVERYTHING up properly to this point, you have now selected and onboarded a self-governing team, one that is culturally and behaviorally locked into the goal of executing and tracking their own daily and weekly activity cadence in a completely transparent fashion. That means you have won more than half the battle. Your

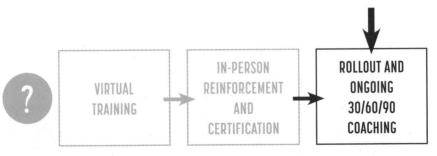

job now is to use strategically timed check-in meetings and coaching sessions with the members of your team. This creates an effective early warning system so that you can communicate effectively both up and down the line exactly what needs to happen for the company to grow revenue aggressively—this quarter and every quarter.

The key concept for the leader to uphold, model, and inspire others with is open collaboration in both directions. That's what turns the Success Cadence from theory into reality: the kind of collaboration in which everything is aboveboard, and there is, by mutual agreement, nowhere to hide. There is no going off in a corner to work on your stuff. Each team member needs to be fully transparent and fully accountable in all their conversations with you about exactly what is in process, how far along it is, and why its projected timeline for closure is realistic. By the same token, you need to be equally transparent and accountable in your conversations with the executive team about exactly the same issues. This principle must be observed continually, to the degree that the instant your CEO/ founder decides they want to look closely at any one individual sales-person's specific status, that can and does happen on the same day. That's what "nowhere to hide" means in action.

Because we're talking about moving the individual activity cadence into the sales team's (and, by extension, the entire organiza-tion's) operational cadence, the way you choose to use your calendar is going be the key to making the principle of open collaboration work. Let's look at how it plays out, first using the example of a smaller sales team, and then moving up to the example of a signifi-cantly larger one.

Example: Freedonia Group

You'll recall the (fictional) Freedonia Group, from earlier in the book. The sales leader there, Kevin, had a moment of truth decision to make about a strong contributor, Paul, who had entitlement issues. After letting Paul go, Kevin worked together with his CEO Diane to make made it a priority to implement the Success Cadence at Freedonia.

Back in Chapter 20, we shared this calendar with you:

The Sales Leader's Quarterly Deliverables

Q1

- Weeks 1–4: Kickoff, Q1 Reality Check
- Week 4: Face-to-Face with CEO
- Weeks 6–13: Deliver on Q1 Forecast

Q2

- Weeks 1–4: Q2 Reality Check
- Week 4: Face-to-Face with CEO
- Weeks 6–13: Deliver on Q2 Forecast

Q3

- Weeks 1–4: Q3 Reality Check
- Week 4: Face-to-Face with CEO
- Weeks 6–13: Deliver on Q3 Forecast

Q4

- Weeks 1–4: Q4 Reality Check
- Week 4: Face-to-Face with CEO
- Weeks 6–13: Deliver on Q4 Forecast

This is the model for the sales leader's quarterly deliverables at comparatively small companies like Freedonia—privately held firms where there is a single sales leader reporting to a single CEO/founder, a small executive team (in Freedonia's case, it's Diane, Kevin, and Jeannette, who serves as both head of accounting and head of operations), and no board of directors. Let's take a look at how Kevin used this calendar of quarterly deliverables to create an operational success cadence at Freedonia.

Freedonia, Revisited

After Paul's departure, Kevin started over with a blank slate. He spent most of the month of December setting up the tools and resources of his new virtual training program. Kevin decided to conduct his reinforcement and certification boot camp in the second week of January. There were five brand-new sales hires and 19 current staff. Everyone was scheduled to take part in virtual training right after New Year's Day.

By the time reinforcement and certification concluded, Kevin had confirmed that 18 of his 19 current producers and four out of five of his new hires had successfully completed virtual training and passed probation. He had let go of the other two people, who clearly hadn't established a good fit. For those who remained, he had completed and discussed in depth, during one-on-one sessions with all 23 members of his team, individualized, confidential willing-and-able matrixes he had set up for them. He then let the entire team know that everyone, whether a new hire or someone who had been with the firm for years, should now consider that they were starting over from Day 1. The sales team would be operating differently than it had in the past.

Based on the activity cadences that had been agreed on at boot camp, Kevin set clear, customized weekly and monthly benchmarks for both activity and revenue generation for each individual salesperson who reported to him. He also reminded each member of the team that there would be a working assumption of autonomy and independence if they followed their agreements and met their benchmarks—and quick intervention if they didn't.

Prior to all this, Kevin had identified annual and quarterly revenue targets with Diane. (That had happened at the end of November.) In the third week of January, he began comprehensive reality checks—also known as pipeline reviews—with each of the 23 members of the team. He did this with the aim of determining whether that Q1 income target he and Diane had discussed was in fact achievable.

After surveying where each team member really was in terms of pipeline, Kevin came up with a projection he felt confident about: the current team would hit only 95% of the Q1 target.

He didn't sugar-coat this information. He didn't hide it. He didn't bury it in the bottom of a long email. At his scheduled one-on-one commitment meeting with Diane during the fifth week of Q1, he discussed the real situation openly, sharing all the information from all 23 individual projections. There was complete transparency.

Together, Kevin and Diane reviewed the situation and concluded that it would make sense for Kevin to onboard one more salesperson that quarter: Melanie. Melanie had been on Kevin's radar screen for some time; after Paul's sudden exit he had committed to developing a bench of sales talent that he could bring on board as circumstances required—and hiring her was what circumstances now required.

Kevin agreed to conduct virtual training and hold one-on-one meetings with Melanie to bring her up to speed with the other members of the team, thereby setting up a personalized kickoff sequence for this critical new hire. (In addition to this, of course, Kevin was also committed to brief weekly check-ins with all of the other members of the team and to in-depth one-on-one monthly coaching sessions for each of them around the 30-day, 60-day, and 90-day points of Q1.)

Later on the same day of his face-to-face meeting with Diane, Kevin took part in her quarterly operations meeting. This was a meeting involving the three senior executives at Freedonia—Diane, Kevin, and Jeannette, the head of accounting, who also served as de facto vice president of operations. The three of them reviewed Kevin's sales forecast for Q1 and confirmed that it made financial sense to hire and onboard an additional salesperson immediately. Again, all the relevant information was available to everyone. If Jeannette needed details on how far a specific deal that was being pursued by one of the members of the sales team had progressed, she got that information.

Having completed both his quarterly commitment face-to-face meeting with Diane and the operations meeting with her and Jeannette, Kevin now had the resources he needed—the budget to hire and onboard Melanie. He also had a clear personal responsibility to deliver 100% of the Q1 target. That's what he and his team did.

Why It Works

That, then, is how the Success Cadence plays out over a single quarter on a smaller sales team. We have seen this cycle play out ourselves many times. It works.

Notice why it works: Kevin isn't making vague assurances about the viability of the Q1 sales target based on his own, or his team's, unquantifiable emotions of optimism and enthusiasm. Instead, he's getting into the hard-number details of each salesperson's pipeline, looking closely at both the leading indicators (activity and sales process milestones) and lagging indicators (closed business). He's using those indicators to create a statistically defensible forecast for each and every one of them—a forecast that he can stand behind. He's then making available all of the details of all of the forecasts to both Diane and Jeannette and creating staffing recommendations based on that information. Diane and Jeannette don't have to review all 23 individual forecasts if they don't want to, but they can if they need to. Just as there is nowhere for Kevin's salespeople to hide, Kevin himself is not looking for any hiding place. Everything his team is doing is out on the table.

Notice, too, that this routine is calendar-driven. The quarterly reality-check meetings always take place in the first four weeks of the Freedonia quarter. The face-to-face commitment and operations meetings always take place in Week 5. Weeks 6–13 are always devoted to hitting the Q1 revenue target confirmed during the critical one-on-one meetings with Diane.

What's the engine for all of that production? You already know that. It's the daily and weekly activity cadence each of Kevin's salespeople committed to in writing. That's what moves the whole team forward. If that rhythm stops, the company's momentum stops.

Let's look now at how the Success Cadence unfolds at a much larger organization by examining another (fictional) situation.

Example: Sales Leadership Sets the Cadence for Huxley Systems

Huxley Systems is a global leader in inventory management software. Qasim is Huxley's CEO. Barbara is its chief revenue officer—the organization's sales leader.

Huxley has three geographical divisions: North America, Asia/Pacific, and Europe. Each of those geographical operating divisions breaks down into a number of regional subdivisions. For the sake of simplicity, we'll focus on the North American division, which has the following regional subdivisions: East, Central, West, and Canada. The East subdivision happens to include five local selling teams: Atlanta, Charlotte, Philadelphia, Boston, and New York. Our illustration will zero in on the New York team, which is led by Alexandria.

Huxley's Success Cadence, like Freedonia's, is based on a repeatable quarterly pattern of activity. That activity, like Freedonia's, is driven by a weekly and annual activity cadence that's committed to, in writing, by the front-line salespeople in (for instance) the New York office. Just as the Freedonia sequence is built to prepare Kevin to give Diane, his CEO, and Jeannette, his finance lead, verifiable quarterly forecasts during their Week 5 quarterly meetings, the Huxley sequence is built to get verifiable forecast data into the hands of the key people in the organization, early in the quarter.

Huxley has a quarterly board of directors meeting at Week 8 of every quarter. The big question for Barbara, in designing her far-flung global team's cadence, is: "How do I get accurate information about this quarter's performance into Qasim's hands at least two weeks before his meeting with the board of directors?"

The key word there is "accurate." Barbara isn't talking about getting hopeful information about the current quarter into Qasim's hands. By the same token, she's not talking about getting a forecast that's easy to exceed into Qasim's hands. She's talking about a verifiable, real-world projection that Qasim, or any of her colleagues, can stress-test at any point of their choosing. Just like Kevin, her goal is to put everything on the table. But since her organization is a good deal larger than Kevin's, there are a number of additional steps she and her global team need to take.

Like Kevin, Barbara has an agreed-upon revenue target for Q1. Unlike Kevin, she has a number of geographical and regional managers to work with. Fortunately, all of them are working on an operating cadence that syncs up with Barbara's reporting requirements. Here's how that operating cadence breaks down.

During Week 2 of Q1, regional manager Alexandria in New York conducts reality checks with her team, confirming whether her people will hit the portion of the company revenue goal they've accepted and are willing to be held accountable for. In particular, she looks at the progress report of a major deal her team is pursuing: the HugeCo account. This is a complex deal that involves multiple salespeople and multiple tech people, one that has been in process for months. The projected value of the HugeCo account is $20 million over two years. Alexandria examines this opportunity and everything in every team member's pipeline with the same rigor, the same commitment to carefully evaluate both leading and lagging indicators, and the same expectation of full transparency that every leader in the Huxley organization has made part of the working culture.

Alexandria's counterparts in Atlanta, Charlotte, Philadelphia, and Boston are doing the same thing.

By the beginning of Week 3, all the local offices have developed visible and defensible forecasts and have shared them with the East region sales leader, Ezra. Note that, at any point in this chain, Ezra can zoom in as close as he wants on the details of any given deal being worked on by any team member in Atlanta, Charlotte, Philadelphia, Boston, or New York. In other words, Alexandria doesn't simply email a single figure to Ezra that she feels good about in terms of Q1 performance. She opens the books and shares all the relevant information about every deal she has been discussing with her team. It's up to Ezra how deeply he dives into the data supplied by New York (or any of the other local offices).

At the end of Week 3, Ezra, the East region sales leader, takes part in a videoconference led by Stephanie, the leader of the North American division of Huxley. This is Stephanie's opportunity to stress-test the forecasts being provided, not only by Ezra, but by the leaders of the West, Central, and Canadian regions, as well. Here again, Stephanie can dive as deeply or as superficially as she wants into the data provided by the sales leaders who report to her. Everything is on the table. There is nowhere to hide—and no one is interested in hiding. The key question everyone is committed to answering accurately during the regional reality-check call is: "What are we willing to be held accountable for North America delivering in terms of revenue by March 31?" In parallel conference calls that take place around the same time, the leadership teams for Asia/Pacific and Europe examine the same question from their perspective.

In Week 4, Huxley holds its annual kickoff event for the entire sales team, during which everyone aligns on the goals, strategies, and resources that support the coming year. Among the attendees are Huxley's 45 newest salespeople—15 from North America, 15 from Asia/Pacific, and 15 from Europe—who have just completed virtual training and reinforcement and certification. This annual all-team kickoff gathering happens only once a year. This year, it takes place in San Francisco. Alexandria and all the local team leaders are there, as are all their direct reports, all the regional leaders, and the leaders of the North American, Asian/Pacific, and European divisions. And, of course, Barbara is there, too.

At Week 5, Barbara leads a conference call with the leaders of the three geographical divisions. At this point, they've given themselves all the time they need to examine all the activity, review all the forecasts, and create a formal revenue forecast for Huxley's first quarter. During the call, Barbara examines their work and asks questions about the key deliverables. Once again—Barbara has access to all the information about every open deal being pursued by every team. She can dive as deeply as she wants.

As it happens, Barbara has some questions about the HugeCo account. Before she incorporates HugeCo into the Q1 forecast she will deliver to Qasim, she wants to discuss the most recent developments in that opportunity with the two New York salespeople who are working on it: Trudy and Jim. Barbara asks Alexandria to get Trudy and Jim to call her after the leadership call concludes. Alexandria agrees to ask her direct reports Trudy and Jim to reach out to her boss Barbara—and they do. Based on what she hears from them, Barbara opts to keep the projection for HugeCo's closing into the Q1 forecast. The moral here is an important one: The fact that the salespeople report to Alexandria does not mean Barbara can't talk to them. She can and will call whomever she needs to call, throughout the sales organization, to ask any question she deems necessary. So, for that matter, can Qasim, the CEO. Both Barbara and Qasim can also sit in on any sales or leadership call to gauge the willingness and ability of the participants and to engage in the interaction personally. In great companies, these discussions are not just for inspection, but are also opportunities for high-level coaching and for senior executive participation on sales calls, as appropriate. Your people should welcome this level of engagement, whether it is regular or sporadic.

"I wouldn't ask anyone to do anything I wouldn't do myself."

—INDRA NOOYI, CEO, PEPSICO

In Week 6, Barbara reports for her face-to-face executive team meeting with Qasim and the other senior leaders of the organization: the VP of Finance, the VP of Operations, the VP of Product Development, and the VP of Marketing. Qasim asks Barbara to lead the meeting—and she does. She not only shares the Q1 forecast that Qasim will pass along to the board of directors, but she also confirms, with the VP of Finance, the priorities for her Q2 hiring goals (she wants to add 20 new salespeople next quarter) and she makes important revisions to the marketing and production plans for Q2—with Qasim's blessing. By the way, we should note here that these discussions must take place in real time, ideally face-to-face. Emailing spreadsheets is not enough. Many CRM tools provide great data views, and some have superb analytical engines that can, when used properly, forecast business outcomes better than the field team. This is a fantastic way to get different views of the pipeline, and the right CRM program can bring validity to the numbers you're working with. Even the best data analysis, however, is not a substitute for real-time, voice-to-voice interactions among the people and teams responsible for strategizing deal-by-deal dynamics.

Qasim now has the hard information he needs for a successful meeting with the board of directors in Week 8. That's because Barbara's carefully designed operational cadence drives not only the sales team's calendar but the calendar of the entire organization.

Take a look at Barbara's quarterly calendar now. Notice that it parallels Kevin's (much simpler) calendar—and that, like Kevin's calendar, it is easily repeatable in Q2, Q3, and Q4, using the same basic structure to deliver open collaboration in both directions. (The only exception there is the all-team kickoff meeting, which happens only in Q1.)

Week 1		
Week 2	Team/Regional Reality Checks	
Week 3	Regional Forecasts Completed	Geographical (North America, Asia/Pacific, Europe) Reality Checks
Week 4	Initial Q1 Executive Forecast Completed	Annual Kickoff Event in San Francisco
Week 5	Geographical (North America, Asia/Pacific, Europe) Leaders Review Executive Forecast with Chief Revenue Officer (CRO)	
Week 6	Q1 Executive Forecast Updated	Executive Team Meeting: CEO, CRO, VP of Finance, VP of Operations, VP of Product Development

Week 7		
Week 8	Company Update: CEO meets with Board of Directors	
Week 9		
Week 10		
Week 11	Final Q1 Executive Forecast Submitted	Executive Team Meeting: CEO, CRO, VP of Finance, VP of Operations, VP of Product Development
Week 12		
Week 13		

What They Have in Common

Small companies that implement the Success Cadence have three important traits in common with big companies that do so. These three things are your critical takeaways for this chapter. Study them closely.

"The question isn't who's going to let me; it's who is going to stop me."

—AYN RAND, AMERICAN AUTHOR

Key Takeaways

- First, the company's top leadership works with real numbers that can be stress-tested—not best guesses. Typically, field teams are left to their own devices, and their leaders are asked to generate estimates or projections that do not connect to anything tangible that the executive team can evaluate independently. That's the exact opposite of what happens in a Success Cadence operation. Because everyone is committed to the principles of transparency and open collaboration in both directions, there is nowhere to hide. Success Cadence companies don't make estimates that are based on hunches or daydreams. They make them based on the hard data and the viable activity trajectories established by their individual salespeople.

- Second, the organizational focus is on setting up an early warning system. If there's going to be a problem meeting the quarterly numbers, leadership needs to know about it early in the quarter, while there is still time to do something about it. Sabotaging the early warning system—by consciously feeding information into it that isn't complete and accurate—is a fireable offense.

- Third, the sales leader, working in collaboration with the CEO/founder, is in the operational driver's seat. This is nonnegotiable, and applies directly to your relationships with people in Marketing and Product Development. We've seen too many situations where a sales leader sits quietly during executive team meetings and accepts whatever Product Development and Marketing gives them, regardless of the quality of the output and regardless of the disruptions these initiatives create in the field. This is a momentum killer—and a company killer. Sales leaders must have the courage to stand up for the right approach. If that means rejecting marketing collateral, so be it. If that means changing production schedules, so be it. The Success Cadence is pragmatic in nature, highly planned, and collaborative, but it is always—repeat, always—led by the sales leader. It is a sad but unavoidable fact of business life that people from Marketing and Product Development, in particular, have a bad habit of jumping all over their organizations and making decisions that negatively impact the sales side with little or no consultation. You and your CEO must establish common cause against this pattern. Marketing and Product Development initiatives must fit into the sales leaders' cadence, rather than creating disruption in a sound operating rhythm in the field.

Your Commitment

- Create a second draft of your quarterly calendar.

CHAPTER TWENTY-SEVEN

Talent Assessment Meetings

ONCE A YEAR, THE EXECUTIVE committee must convene to assess the talent that exists in the organization and the leadership team's level of success in attracting and retaining new talent. This is a critical part of the Success Cadence and a core requirement of a rapid-growth culture. As the sales leader, you will and should be evaluated on the number and quality of talented people you've brought into the organization and on the learning and career paths you've established for them. That's what moving up and to the right is all about.

"In times of change, learners inherit the earth, while the learned find themselves beautifully equipped to deal with a world that no longer exists."

–ERIC HOFFER, AMERICAN MORAL AND SOCIAL PHILOSOPHER

Oddly, the individual skill of talent acquisition and development remains (in our experience, anyway) one of the leadership responsibilities that top-level leaders in most companies simply neglect. Most CEOs do not make any effort to evaluate this on an annual basis—or any basis—for the members of the senior leadership team. That makes zero sense. Your organization's ability to attract and hold onto talented people is its ultimate resource and its ultimate competitive advantage. Why in the world wouldn't you pause for just one day out of the year and take stock of who's growing the base of willing and able employees (specifically the base of HiPOs) that needs help in that area and how well the company as a whole is doing when it comes to aggressively expanding its talent base?

This is the natural culmination of all the work you have done during the year to attract, hire, and retain willing-and-able contributors. As part of your quarterly review sessions with your direct reports, you will identify the top performers, the people who need help, and the people who do not represent a good fit and who need to be gracefully transitioned off the team. This is the essence of the quarterly review process.* Working on the same quarterly cadence, you will create appropriate learning paths for each direct report,

---

* You yourself, as a sales leader, will also undergo the same kind of review. It should be conducted annually by your CEO/founder.

and you will identify the high-potential leadership contributors—HiPOs—whom you brought into the organization and who belong on a management track. You will also identify people on your team who present special skills that don't necessarily connect to team leadership (content development, for example) and set up appropriate learning paths—and career paths—for them. You will do all this based on hard numbers, using clear metrics to chart the willing-and-able trajectories of everyone who reports to you.

The one-day talent assessment meeting is where you get your personal report card on how well you've done the talent acquisition and development component of your job. In the beginning, it will be your CEO giving you feedback on the level and volume of the talent you personally have brought in the door and nurtured. As your organization grows, the full-day discussion will expand to include all the sales leaders who report directly to you, who also have the responsibility to secure and retain top talent. Ultimately, this process spreads to all functions in the organization—not just sales—and the talent discussion becomes cross-functional. We have seen many, many examples of great talent identified and moved to higher value positions based on these discussions. Imagine the potential upward company trajectory when the willing-and-able culture transcends functions.

As salespeople are accountable for the book of business they create and sustain on a weekly, monthly, quarterly, and annual basis, so are you accountable for the talent you bring into the company during the same calendar periods. That's not just sales talent—it's all the talent you track on your radar screen, maintain an ongoing relationship with, recruit to your team, and (gasp!) even transfer to another department when they have a hole to fill and you have the person on staff who best fills it.

Just as a salesperson wouldn't walk in the door for a quarterly review session without any activity or any pipeline to point to, you don't want to walk into this meeting without any talented hires, viable career paths, and well-planned learning paths to point to.

Key Takeaway

- Use this full-day talent assessment session to evaluate the past, assess the present, and plan for the future in terms of the development of your company's talent base. Identify the rising stars. Identify the next generation of leaders. Identify key talent. Then, set up a clear plan to support them.

Your Commitment

- You now have a clear sense of all the elements of the Success Cadence. In the next section of the book, we will share some insights on implementation that will be helpful to you and to your executive team as you move forward. So continue to Part 3, "From Slow Growth to Rapid Growth."

Part 3:
From Slow Growth
to Rapid Growth

CHAPTER TWENTY-EIGHT

The 15 Pain Points of a Slow-Growth Culture

IT IS LIKELY THAT YOU will be implementing the Success Cadence within a company that is already up and running, which is another way of saying that you will be attempting to put into practice what we have shared with you here within an organization that does not yet have a rapid-growth workplace culture in place. That means you are going to encounter pushback and operational obstacles that are rooted in the conventional wisdom common in companies where there is a prevailing slow-growth working culture. In this chapter, we examine 15 of the most common symptoms of such a culture, which are best understood as growing pains. We also offer you some insights on how to address the underlying problems so that you can move past the pain point and implement the program we've outlined for you and your executive committee in the earlier chapters.

Pain Point 1: Entitlement Mindset

Loosely translated, this means, "I deserve special treatment, better pay, more perks, and more attention than others. I also am allowed to subordinate company interests in favor of my own." The entitlement mindset is a failure of accountability. When executives allow an unaccountable culture to take root or, even worse, endorse it with their personal example, a toxic dynamic spreads and the company comes last. An outlook of entitlement means the person in question—whatever their title—is not willing to support the we-first working culture.

Conventional Wisdom

- "Young and aggressive is good."
- "As long as only a few people are doing this, it's OK."
- "We hire fast." (Not necessarily smart!)
- "If something goes wrong, it's HR's fault."
- "Some people get to ignore agreements."

The Reality

- Top leadership may be modeling the entitlement mindset. If this continues, rapid sales growth is too expensive—both from a financial and a cultural point of view—and eventually unsustainable.
- If there is the mindset of entitlement on the sales force, there is likely no hiring profile for the role and no effective hiring

process in place. The sales leader must own this and must be held accountable.

- The entitlement mindset usually reveals that there are no clear lines on why people do or don't have to follow the rules, and therefore most rules have no impact.

- It becomes difficult if not impossible to get good analytics on the business with this mindset. People with entitlement issues typically are reluctant to share information; they play everything close to the vest.

- If this is left unchecked, the concept of we-first is destroyed, leading to a culture of me-first and a downward performance spiral. When everyone is looking out for number one, no one is looking out for the company.

What to Do

- Create a defined willing-and-able success profile for the role and build the recruiting, hiring, and onboarding process around it.

- Eliminate patterns of entitled behavior at the top level of the organization.

- Create clear standards and expectations during team meetings (without singling people out). Point out certain behaviors, then connect the dots as to why a given behavior doesn't support the team's mission and objectives, what it means to the company and to mutual success, and what the consequences are if the behavior isn't changed.

- Meet privately with those who report to you who have

entitlement issues, and go over your specific expectations. Don't assume everyone knows what moving up and to the right looks like.

- Reward accountability as a way of doing business and a way of life.
- Part company gracefully with those who insist on being me-first.

Pain Point 2: Unaligned Messaging from Top Leadership

If you lead a team and identify a priority, you must make sure your actions and decisions support that priority. Some executives routinely assume the right to send messages that are totally incongruent with their actions and decisions. This behavioral example creates confusion throughout the organization as to what the objectives and initiatives really are, and thus becomes a major inhibitor to a rapid-growth culture.

Conventional Wisdom

- "If it's on my mind right now, it must be important and worth saying to everyone."
- "They're smart enough to figure it out."
- "Front-line management can translate what I mean."
- "I'm the boss, and I can change the priorities or pivot without repercussions downstream."

The Reality

- When this happens consistently, no one listens to the CEO

anymore, or some people listen and go in one direction, while others don't listen and go in another. As this dynamic makes its way onto teams, a blight starts to spread throughout the organization.

What to Do

- The leader of the company needs to get clear on their own job description. The senior executive's job is to clearly outline the mission/purpose, the vision, and the specific objectives. Functional executives need to communicate their initiatives to support those objectives. They can only hold their people accountable when there are no mixed messages from the top, when leaders adopt a high-road mentality and hold themselves to the highest standards, and when messaging from the top is supported by action that connects the dots.

- Use an annual all-team kickoff event to clarify the corporate objective, the business strategy that supports the objective, the funded initiatives that support the strategy, and the obstacles that must be overcome. Yes, planning happens throughout the year at rapid-growth companies, and tweaks may be made along the way, but the kickoff must set the stage.

- If you change the message or the objectives, that needs to be communicated clearly from the top, meaning that the company leader must speak directly about the old and the new objectives and explain why the old is going away and the new is now more important. This requires a high level of management courage, as well as a viable plan that the management team has been consulted on and agrees with.

- Sales leaders: If all else fails, ask the troops for feedback on the disconnected messaging; share this privately with the CEO/founder.

Pain Point 3: Too Many Silos

Unaligned messaging and the lack of a unified operating cadence may lead to a situation where there are organizational silos that typically don't interact or interact ineffectively. This decreases productivity, impedes communication, and makes rapid growth virtually impossible.

Conventional Wisdom

- "If everyone just worries about their group, then that results in the whole company doing well."
- "If my team shines, then the company shines as well."
- "I'm focusing on my own lane."
- "The CEO knows how it all fits together." (Not necessarily!)

The Reality

- Silos with team members who don't interact well (or at all) with the members of other silos negatively impact your organization's ability to grow and scale.

What to Do

- Determine whether the existing organizational groups are

pursuing the same objectives, strategy, and initiatives. If not, align them with the CEO's compass. Consider implementing a cross-functional leadership role that can break down silos through planning, alignment, and collaboration.

- Identify the clearly defined leading and lagging indicators that should be tracked in pursuit of these objectives. Establish them as universal benchmarks.

- Identify new leadership talent via a talent assessment session, and align them with the CEO's compass. Do this sooner rather than later. There is no time to waste.

Pain Point 4: The Great Product/ Service Assumption

This symptom—assuming a great product or service will solve every problem—is often a result of the silo mentality, of unwarranted executive assumptions, or of a combination of the two. Simple hubris often plays a role. Company founders may have difficulty understanding why anyone wouldn't want their product. They often assume that the sales team simply doesn't know how to sell it, when in fact there are any number of other potential issues to address.

Conventional Wisdom

- "More product training and marketing will increase sales."
- "Superior product wins the battle every time."
- "We don't have to have high-priced salespeople when the product sells itself."

- "If the product did not sell, that's clearly an execution issue that can be fixed by replacing the head of sales."

The Reality

- Even a great product/service needs a plan and coordinated action to succeed in the marketplace or to succeed to its potential.
- Great salespeople are just as important as a great product. Someone needs to connect the needs of the buyer to the features of the product.

What to Do

- Get feedback from buyers on the business problems the product solves and on future innovation ideas.
- Use this information to identify for the sales team the key facts about the product, what it does, where the market is, who the likely buyer is, what the typical pain is and its dollar cost, what the typical gain is once the product is implemented, why your product/service is better than alternatives, and what the verifiable business case benefits are—including proof of when and where you have done it.
- The sales team must be able to spot the elements that can turn a lead into a prospect. Identify those and the qualification questions that uncover them.
- Listen carefully to what sales is uncovering about the product/ service experience from direct interactions with customers— and act on it. Sales cannot be held accountable for such issues

as technical challenges within the product, poor design, or long timeframes to deliver value to customers due to over-complexity, all of which are common in industries such as high-tech and pharmaceuticals. The leadership challenge lies in ensuring that product and development teams spot and resolve those issues expeditiously; if the problems go unresolved for extended periods, top sales talent will move on to other organizations—perhaps to a direct competitor.

Pain Point 5: Doing the Sales Team's Job

Many sales "managers" end up doing a significant portion of the selling for which their team is supposedly responsible.

> *"Taking initiative pays off. It is hard to visualize someone as a leader if she is always waiting to be told what to do."*
>
> **–SHERYL SANDBERG, COO, FACEBOOK**

Conventional Wisdom

- "I have to help them put out fires."
- "If they ask me for help, I need to help."
- "So-and-so will blow the deal if I don't get involved."

The Reality

- If your insight, advice, and personal support is required for resolving most, or even a sizable portion, of the issues the sales team encounters, you are supporting a culture of learned helplessness.

- A pattern of constant heroics on your side may make you feel good, but it doesn't grow your team and it doesn't do anything but plateau your contributions to the company.

What to Do

- Build and defend appropriate guardrails. If you were managing a team of just three or four people, you might be able to get away with swooping in like a superhero every time a salesperson needed your advice on how to close a deal, soothe a ruffled prospect, resolve a problem with other teams within your organization, or plan a major presentation. But you're not managing three or four people. So the question is: Does it really make sense for all the team's problem-solving roads to lead through you? Here's a hint: No.

- The advice your team members request from you, even with the best of intentions, is often an attempt to get you to do their job—and that's neither scalable or sustainable. What you're after is a working culture in which people act as if they own the company, within narrowly defined areas. They must have the autonomy and support they need from you to make the best independent decisions possible, while driving within the guardrails you identify for them and appropriately influencing colleagues in other roles. They should be able to work across functional lines to get their job done without having to check with you. Only in this way can your team be expected to become self-governing and scalable.

- Here's the deal you want to strike: If the salesperson stays within the guardrails you define, they get to act independently—and, yes, mess up from time to time, tell you exactly what happened, and learn from the mistake. That way of doing business may take some getting used to on both sides, but really, what's the alternative? You wind up with a team driven by learned helplessness that puts all the pressure on you—and squanders everyone's precious time.

- Live the cadence. As you know, each member of your team should have a daily and weekly activity cadence that sets out exactly what needs to happen, and when, in order for the person to hit their revenue targets. The activity cadence should be written down, personalized to each salesperson, and subject to regular review and analysis by both you and your direct report.

- Guess what? You, too, need an activity cadence. How much time each week are you committing to spend on recruiting? On weekly in-person catch-up meetings? On in-depth coaching sessions? On ride-alongs? On meetings with senior management and strategic partners? All of this needs to be quantified and set down in writing, too. Don't improvise it. Your commitment to design and follow through on your own personal activity cadence is just as important as your direct reports' commitment to follow theirs. Everyone on your team—including you—must establish this kind of daily and weekly activity rhythm. Your own daily and weekly time investments should be just as conscious, strategically sound, and predictable as those of your team.

Pain Point 6: Ineffective Hiring and Recruiting

The sales team's culture lives or dies with your talent acquisition model. When a sales team has pockets of an entitlement mindset or polarization between groups of producers (or people in other functions), that means the hiring and recruiting model is flawed and the culture is being sabotaged. This symptom is typically rooted in a lack of, or fear of, diversity. It is a direct result of poor leadership (for example, "I know talent when I see it" when the data doesn't support that) and is worsened by the silo mentality and, not infrequently, by simple panic from the top of the organization.

Conventional Wisdom

- "Winners stick out, and I can spot them."
- "Great people find us."
- "We hire outside firms to hire great people."
- "We get all our people from my last company." (This signals a diversity-of-thought problem.)
- "Our job descriptions filter out people who shouldn't be here."
- "We're too busy to be in hiring mode all the time."
- "So-and-so is a known performer." (When actually, so-and-so is a friend of someone who works at the company.)

The Reality

- Bad hires set the company back exponentially. They are too expensive, in terms of money, attention, and lost opportunity to justify even once.

What to Do

- Whenever bad hires happen in any area of the organization (not just sales), acknowledge the mistake, off-board the person tactfully, and fix what was broken in the recruitment and hiring process.
- Always be hiring; always be developing.
- Follow the guidelines discussed in Chapter 23.
- Emphasize diversity, including but not limited to the racial and gender kind. Hire for diversity of thought, background, and operating style, and support an environment where speaking up and asking questions is encouraged.

"Knowing what must be done
does away with fear."

—ROSA PARKS, AMERICAN CIVIL RIGHTS ACTIVIST

Pain Point 7: Heavy Over-Assignment of Quota

Pressure from other parts of the organization may create sales goals that sales leaders know are unrealistic. When sales leaders don't push back, this demoralizes the team, masks the real problems, and is a signal of potentially catastrophic disconnect between the front lines and the senior executive team. It ends up being a race to the bottom: "I make your quota more and more unachievable, and you demand more and more salary to make up for it—or you quit, and we end up with a lot of B-level players."

Conventional Wisdom

- "Raise the bar and expectations, and people will produce more."
- "They fall short anyway, so why not raise the bar so when they do fall short they are closer to our goal number?"
- "It saves us money if we over-assign."
- "More marketing produces more sales."
- "Sales will probably never know that we over-assigned by this much—and even if the sales team collectively falls short, we executives will still make our bonus."

The Reality

- Unrealistic quotas are demotivating to the sales team. Period. They drive away top sales talent. Senior executives, specifically CFOs, need to recognize this. All too often, they don't.
- We've seen situations where major public companies published wildly unrealistic income projections based on aggressive sales targets. They did so even knowing that literally no one—as in zero people—on the sales team made quota the last time around. What in the world makes the higher number more attainable? This level of denial and top-down thinking is a sign of a dysfunctional working culture.

What to Do

- Work with the CEO and the CFO to create a compensation plan that maps effectively to your market and your sales team. Spend some time on this. You don't have to bust the budget if you invest the time necessary to model the compensation plan effectively and aim to create a system that is simple enough for salespeople not to be tempted to game it.

- Set revenue goals collaboratively, with all the open communication necessary in both directions. Create real-time collaboration between Sales and Finance on ascending growth targets relative to quota carriers entering the business and ramping up to full productivity to sell effectively.
- Avoid peaks and valleys in hiring; they contribute to peaks and valleys in revenue. Make linearity king.

Pain Point 8: Too Much or Not Enough Process

Teams operating in slow-growth cultures often get stuck in one of these extremes, typically as a result of management fear ("I won't or can't get buy-in") or lack of skill ("I'll add a ton of process hoping something sticks").

Conventional Wisdom

- "Don't bog down the troops with process."
- "We know what we are doing and don't need to be micromanaged. Process doesn't help. Corporate is just trying to control what we do as professional sellers."
- "Just make the number."

The Reality

- You can't scale without a viable common framework.
- No baseline means you will spin rather than improve. Too much process means gridlock. Just enough process, aligned

with the right tools and the proper operational cadence, maximizes both achievement and autonomy.

What to Do

- Audit each group to look for processes that everyone agrees can be improved.
- Ask new people where you have too much or not enough process in place—use this as a starting point.
- Aim for common process, common vocabulary, and common tools throughout the sales organization. (A training and development partner can help you with this.)
- Let salespeople know that you'll target your coaching to those areas that matter most to success within their role at this moment and this period of time. (Salespeople really do hate to be micromanaged.)
- Design for everyone. If the process does not improve performance in multiple selling roles, you've failed in design. Creating a process to benefit a single person or team at the expense of others is a death trap.
- Quantify prior process improvements and prove there was a return to them; communicate what you've learned about the returns on improvements to those responsible for compliance.

Pain Point 9: Disparity in Headcount Allocation

Growing the organization at disparate rates is a classic mistake that arises from the first four symptoms on this list. You must support the organization strategically as it scales. For instance:

If your salespeople need technical support in order to hit their sales goals, your headcounts on new teams must take this into account. In addition, as the organization scales, new roles need to be added that were never part of the early stage organization (for instance trainers, business value consultants, and best-practices coordinators/advocates).

Conventional Wisdom

- "Sell first, then staff."
- "Let the current support staff handle it until they can't do any more—then expand complementary support roles. "
- "Staff will eventually speak up."

The Reality

- When you don't staff properly, you suboptimize your value delivery, make your customers unhappy, jeopardize follow-on sales, and increase churn. New people can't get up to speed fast enough since they're putting out fires. Revenues from new and existing customers suffer.

What to Do

- Find out your ideal staffing ratios and apply them to the growth phase as well. Whenever you see that your success ratings are declining, add complementary support personnel. Do not expect salespeople to pick up the slack. They won't.
- Establish the proper ratios by means of an ongoing real-time conversation involving Sales, Operations, and Finance. Don't

put off this conversation. If you don't model and discuss the ratios and pursue the right people pipeline in real time, you will fall behind and find it difficult or impossible to recover momentum.

Pain Point 10: Using CRM Systems in a Vacuum

This symptom typically expresses itself in someone outside of sales making nonnegotiable demands for information in CRM without engaging in human-to-human dialogue. These blind demands typically do not support the sales team and can cause resentment and massive non-compliance.

Conventional Wisdom

- "The numbers and information in the CRM funnel should be accurate, and they're not. If the sales team just complied, we would already have the information we need."
- "We can't get accurate information from the salespeople."
- From the sales team: "Entering CRM and opportunity details slows us down. Stop taking time out of our selling efforts."

The Reality

- CRM data integrity is an issue in every organization to some degree or another.
- The big myth on CRM is that if only the sales team would comply with using it, the company would have all the information it needs. The reality is that there is inevitably a lot of data

cleanup that needs to take place and that other teams need to be a part of it. Salespeople need to see more benefit from the CRM than just the cost of data entry.

What to Do

- Err on the side of not asking for too much. What specific information do you want as an output from CRM that is critical to making data-driven decisions that support your mission and objectives as a company? That's what should be discussed and hashed out. Then, you can sort out the minimum required from the sales team that gives them good value for their time. If you ask them to input more, even if it's, say, a simple drop-down box with a picklist of competitors, what can you ask them to do less of? What do you really need, based on this year's objectives?

- Hold the sales team accountable for updating the CRM based on the sales process and for using the CRM to distinguish qualified opportunities from everything else. If a salesperson knows how to sell your product, then they know what has to happen within a defined period of time in order for revenue to be predictable. If they cannot manage to disclose this information transparently to internal people who need it, the assumption must be that they don't understand or don't want to disclose the status of the opportunity in question and its ability to close within a predictable period of time. Withholding this information is a basic failure of willing-and-able performance requirements, specifically those regarding sales process, analytics focus, and transparency.

Pain Point 11: Faulty Analytics/Lack of Data Discipline

This symptom involves making decisions without data, having the right data and not doing anything with it, or looking at the data you have rather than the data you need. If you don't have the information you need to make a good decision, get it. The rapid-growth culture is always data-driven. Note that the effects of this symptom are inevitably worsened by a silo mentality.

Conventional Wisdom

- "I know this business."
- "Based on the information we have, we make great decisions."
- "We have 20 pages of KPIs that tell us all we need to know about our business."
- "Any bad decision can be fixed if acted on quickly."

The Reality

- What you need is the right data that is accurate, timely, and aligned with your targeted goals and objectives. Everything else is noise that slows you down.
- When you make decisions without the right data, you are flying blind, wasting precious capital, and teaching direct reports to follow your example and make gut instinct the criterion in their own world.

What to Do

- Sit down with the appropriate stakeholders and ask: "What are the things we would like to have to run this corner of our business—that fit in with the CEO's corporate objectives?" Now, go get the best available data in that area and measure it. This is the only way to make informed and defensible decisions that support the business.

Pain Point 12: Delusional Pipeline Syndrome

It's easy to create a false sense of hope, but creating real opportunities that add value to both parties requires a deeper conversation, both inside and outside the sales team. The absence of such conversations connects to the symptom of faulty analytics, as well as to the imposition of an unrealistic quota.

Conventional Wisdom

- "If it's in the pipeline, then we should be able to close it."
- "If we have three times the value of the our targeted plan in the pipeline, we'll be OK."

The Reality

- A delusional pipeline is a cultural issue. It decreases trust between sales and management, causes bad planning on many levels, and reduces the sales team's credibility in the organization. Much of the garbage in the pipeline is the result of management pressure.

While it may feel good to put salespeople under pressure to fill the pipeline, the pressure doesn't do any good.

- Setting an arbitrary standard such as "three times the desired revenue" is meaningless if your team is feeding unqualified contacts and opportunities into the pipeline. (Most teams are.) The actual conversion rates of qualified prospects will be a matter of direct experience within your industry, market, and company. There is no predictable ratio that applies to all situations.

What to Do

- Set revenue goals collaboratively, from the bottom up and the top down, as described in Chapter 22 of this book, with all the open communication necessary in both directions to sustain a productive ongoing dialogue. (Most companies simply take a top-down approach, telling the sales team to "just make the numbers," and then wondering why that doesn't happen predictably.)
- Make "yelling at the scoreboard" culturally unacceptable. (Start with the person in the mirror.)
- Track and discuss leading indicators (activity that is known to result in real opportunities) as closely as you track lagging indicators (closed sales and sales rankings).
- The salesperson's job is to disqualify people who don't belong in the pipeline so take unqualified leads out of the sales pipeline as the sales process moves forward and don't project revenue from them. Some people belong in a structured nurturing process—that's different from being a qualified prospect.

- If there is no mutually-agreed-upon next step in place with a buyer or influencer who can set an appointment to discuss doing business, consider the opportunity unqualified.
- If the discussion's timeframe has exceeded your typical selling cycle, consider the opportunity unqualified.
- If the buyer does not acknowledge that there is a business problem that your organization can solve, consider the opportunity unqualified.
- If the buyer refuses to talk to you about the budget for solving the problem, consider the opportunity unqualified.
- If the buyer will not discuss the decision-making process in place for determining whether or not to buy, consider the opportunity unqualified.

Pain Point 13: Selling Short to Make the Quarter

This extremely common symptom suggests that the sales team may not be aligned with the willing-and-able matrix and the cultural requirements of the job since late-quarter heroics are strongly discouraged in favor of linearity. It may also mean that there is a sales execution problem, a product problem, or a demand problem that no one wants to admit.

Conventional Wisdom

- "Volume makes up for it."
- "Make your number now and create trust with investors—then we can worry about the issue next time."
- "Sell forward at all costs; discount at will; be aggressive."
- "Win the business no matter what."

- "Time will solve this issue."

The Reality

- Salespeople who discount instinctively don't believe the value of their own product/service—or are facing challenges in the market that they know the company doesn't want to address.
- Sales leaders often teach the sales force to discount instinctively, since they know managers will eventually approve the activity (regardless of any lectures to the contrary) and they want their deal done to get their commission.
- Many salespeople—the best, in fact—do not like this practice because it undersells their personal consultative value, hurts their brand, and typically results in less income. If they are forced to sell short by upper management (as sometimes happens), one result is a serious morale problem.

What to Do

- Set realistic expectations.
- Add a modest amount of time to what you think it will take the salesperson to achieve the goal.
- Accept that the plan for a major account may be too aggressive. The fact that someone at AT&T said they liked your idea does not mean AT&T is at 90%.
- Hold the sales team accountable for delivering value, upholding the business model as they do so, and for collaboratively establishing, with the buyer, a clear dollar-value cost of not taking action. How much does it cost, in hard dollars, for the

buyer to maintain the status quo? Remember that everything starts with the business case and the dollar-value benefit of the solution provided to the buyer. Other important factors to consider are issues such as reduced risk to reputation and fewer problems related to compliance and regulation.

- Live by the principle that if the salesperson must discount, they must get something in return for doing so. For instance: the positioning of your product/service to ensure a faster time to value (and not necessarily getting it two days early to meet our quarterly requirements), a warm introduction to a buyer at another company, or a press release. Discounting based on price is a nonstarter.
- Live on facts, not on hope.

Pain Point 14: Not Measuring the Right Business Outcomes

Measuring leads, opportunities, and activities is pointless if you don't measure the outcomes that tie back to the corporate objectives.

Conventional Wisdom

- "More leads will solve all issues."
- "More [euphemism for something that isn't a qualified prospect: trade shows, calls, etc.] will solve our problem."
- "People just need to work harder."
- "You know where you need to be and what you need to pay attention to."

The Reality

- If you can't measure something, then you can't improve it. That definitely applies to your sales process.
- Marketing is often guilty of exacerbating this pain point; they may spend lots of time, effort, and resources collecting trade show leads, downloads, advertising hits, social media likes, or keyword analytics but fail to tie the activity or event in question to a real business outcome. The same goes for salespeople whose networking activity never turns into trackable positive outcomes on their activity cadence commitments.

There is both an art and a science to tying your marketing initiatives to specific business outcomes, and using strong data analytics is an important part of that effort. Gut instinct is not enough. You need the right data. Not everyone can crunch the numbers at the right level of detail, of course, and there is no crime in you not being able to do so—but someone on your team should be able to do the math and help you to make clear connections that are statistically defensible and that everyone on the executive team can agree on.

"Marketing's mission in most companies is to help Sales sell more product to more customers faster and more profitably than Sales could do by itself," said Mark Stouse, CEO of Proof Analytics.

"For this reason, great marketing is a unique multiplier on sales performance, as well as other key aspects of a company like

recruiting and retention. When that marketing impact can't
be proven, it means a lot of volatility, risk and ungoverned
opportunity cost for the company. The C-suite needs to ask the same
questions about marketing they ask about everything in business:
are we investing too much or too little in marketing? If we cut,
what will we lose? If we increase spend, what do we gain? And
how long will it take to see the positive or negative impacts?"

—MARK STOUSE, CEO, PROOF ANALYTICS

What to Do

- Promote and support a culture of data discipline that filters through the rest of the organization.
- Measure the right leading indicators and track their outcomes. Measuring only lagging indicators, such as closed sales, is typical of delusional pipelines and a self-sabotaging mindset.
- Focus your efforts on identifying the perfect target customer. Doing this dramatically increases close rates and has the added benefit of saving your team and your prospect's team tons of time and stress. It also improves the company's reputation— your team won't come off as pushy so often.
- Identify the business outcome of X feature of your product. Identify who benefits from that and who experiences pain when that business outcome is not delivered. Ask yourself: "How can we connect the dots between our product and the customer's ultimate business outcome?"

Pain Point 15: Lack of Training/Misaligned Training Initiatives

Rapid-growth organizations support the development of their people in the short and long terms. The failure to do so is a classic result of crises arising from all the other symptoms on this list. These crises lead some executives to believe that training is not a priority. Actually, the right training initiatives are the solution that will make organizational crises less common and less destructive.

Conventional Wisdom

- "We hire experienced people only."
- "These people don't need training because they've already had it."
- "We trained them last year."
- "Training is the training department's responsibility."
- "Training is the marketing department's responsibility."
- "Training is HR's responsibility."

The Reality

- Unless you invest in, create, and sustain a learning culture, your people will be demotivated, you will not attract the best new talent, and your people will not be equipped to lead when the time comes. You will be mandating a slow-growth working culture and a team composed of B-level contributors who actually may like it with you because there's no pressure to perform. All your best people will leave, however, as they always want to grow and learn.

- You cannot create a learning culture in your organization without training, reinforcement, and coaching. Without a structured and even a very simple training program, you cannot really be assured of tying anything your team does to the company's business objectives.

- On the other hand, if you train and reinforce effectively in hard and soft skills, you raise the bar on retention of your best people and you gain the significant side benefit of bringing up the performance level of your average players while you determine whether to keep them or not. You give them a chance, which improves your brand and your recruiting initiatives.

What to Do

- You should only train your sales team in that which shows up, directly or indirectly, in their willing-and-able matrix. You should regularly train and reinforce them in these elements. While Marketing and HR can and should be engaged for input and potentially some content for your training programs, they should not own this initiative. You, the sales leader, must own it. There can be no competing spin, no other agenda, no other interpretation of what "willing" and "able" mean in the context of your sales team.

- Hold managers accountable for the growth paths of their people.

- Fund training and reinforcement.

- Get explicit buy-in on all this from the executive committee.

In Summary

As you work to implement what we've shared with you in this book, you are going to encounter pushback and operational obstacles that are rooted in the conventional wisdom common in companies where there is a prevailing slow-growth working culture. Don't let it discourage you. Achieving a true rapid-growth Success Cadence is worth it.

Key Takeaways

- This chapter gave you insights on 15 of the most common symptoms of such a culture, which are best understood as growing pains, and suggestions on overcoming each. Use them!

Your Commitment

- Identify which of the 15 pain points accurately describes the state of your organization right now as it prepares to support its Success Cadence initiative. (There are likely several that apply to your world.)

CHAPTER TWENTY-NINE

The Road from Here

AS WE CLOSE THIS BOOK, we remind you (and ourselves) that the Success Cadence never ends. It is always unfolding, always refining and upgrading its aims and resources, always committed to personal and organizational growth, and always finding new corners of the organization to touch and enhance. We've seen entire organizations transformed with the key initiatives led by the sales team that we've shared with you in these pages. We hope you will take on the goal of transforming, not just your sales team, but your entire company.

"No matter how senior you get in an organization, no matter how well you're perceived to be doing, your job is never done."

–ABIGAIL JOHNSON, PRESIDENT AND CEO, FIDELITY INVESTMENTS

We'd like to leave you with two important thoughts. First, the technology you choose to manage this process matters. Although there are any number of platforms and applications that can help you to implement what we've shared with you, we would be remiss in our duty if we didn't mention a powerful software tool for sales teams that is specifically designed to help both leaders and sales teams execute on the willing-and-able matrix, both in the short and the long term. It's called Skillibrium. You can learn more about it by emailing us at SuccessCadence@Sandler.com.

Second, we ask you to bear in mind, as you make this system your own, that any truly successful organization—and any truly successful sales team—is deeply committed to the principle of improving people's lives. We believe that the ideas you've encountered on these pages reflect the best resources and insights now available for making dramatic improvements in the lives of your sales team, your employees, and your customers. If you build your efforts around that principle and share your commitment on that front with the members of your team, you will experience the highest level of success.

We hope you'll keep in touch with us about the results of your work with this system by emailing us at SuccessCadence@sandler.com.

Look for these other books
on shop.sandler.com:

Prospect the Sandler Way
Transforming Leaders the Sandler Way
Selling Professional Services the Sandler Way
Accountability the Sandler Way
Selling Technology the Sandler Way
LinkedIn the Sandler Way
Bootstrap Selling the Sandler Way
Customer Service the Sandler Way
Selling to Homeowners the Sandler Way
Succeed the Sandler Way
The Contrarian Salesperson
The Sales Coach's Playbook
Lead When You Dance
Change the Sandler Way
Motivational Management the Sandler Way
Call Center Success the Sandler Way
Patient Care the Sandler Way
Winning from Failing
Asking Questions the Sandler Way
Why People Buy
Selling in Manufacturing and Logistics
The Road to Excellence
From the Board Room to the Living Room
Making Channel Sales Work
The Unapologetic Saleswoman
The Right Hire
Digital Prospecting
The Art and Skill of Sales Psychology

THE SANDLER RULES
FOR SALES LEADERS
ONLINE COURSE

The definitive resource for effective sales leadership.

This course details 49 sales management principles based on the proven principles of the Sandler Selling System.

If you're like most sales leaders, you may be:

- Frustrated that rogue, "lone wolf" salespeople do things their own way, rather than using the same process as the rest of the team.
- Concerned about creating predictable forecasts and expectations of sales performance.
- Worried about your top-heavy sales force with the top 20% generating 80% of the revenue.

If you want a better team, become a better manager. In this course, you will learn best practices for sales leaders, which you can immediately implement with the members of your team. We will give you an overview of the attitudes, behaviors, and techniques which we have found to be most effective over the past five decades. Dave Mattson, President and CEO of Sandler Training, best-selling author, and world-renown sales leadership expert leads a frank discussion of the strategies and tactics which are most useful to sales managers.

In *Sandler Rules for Sales Leaders,* you will learn how to:

- Eliminate miscommunication
- Hire, onboard, and train top performing salespeople
- Empower your people to succeed without you
- Create a culture of accountability
- And much more!

This video series is based on the best-selling book authored by Dave Mattson. Dave Mattson is a 5-time best-selling author, including *The Sandler Rules* and *The Sandler Rules for Sales Leaders*. He is a global sales and leadership expert. Under his leadership, Sandler Training has grown to over 250 offices in 27 countries around the world.

sandler.com/sales-leaders-rules